SPECIAL REPORTS

ISIS

BY KATIE MARSICO

CONTENT CONSULTANT
Austin Long, PhD
Assistant Professor of International and Public Affairs
Columbia University

Essential Library

An Imprint of Abdo Publishing | abdopublishing.com

abdopublishing.com

Published by Abdo Publishing, a division of ABDO, PO Box 398166, Minneapolis,
Minnesota 55439. Copyright © 2016 by Abdo Consulting Group, Inc. International
copyrights reserved in all countries. No part of this book may be reproduced in
any form without written permission from the publisher. Essential Library™ is a
trademark and logo of Abdo Publishing.

Printed in the United States of America, North Mankato, Minnesota
082015
012016

Cover Photo: Medyan Dairieh/ZumaPress/Corbis
Interior Photos: Ropi/ZumaPress/Newscom, 4–5; Department of Defense, 11; Al
Jazeera/AP Images, 12–13; Emad Matti/AP Images, 18; Militant Video/AP Images,
21; Karim Kadim/AP Images, 23; Hussein Malla/AP Images, 24–25; Fadi al-Halabi/
AFP/Getty Images, 29; Polaris/Newscom, 32; Stringer/Iraq/Reuters/Corbis, 35; AP
Images, 36–37, 89; Lefteris Pitarakis/AP Images, 43; Seivan Selim/AP Images, 47;
STR/EPA/Corbis, 48–49; Mike Theiler/Picture-Alliance/DPA/AP Images, 51; Matt
Cetti-Roberts/ZumaPress/Corbis, 57; Gail Orenstein/NurPhoto/Sipa USA/AP Images,
59; Steven Senne/AP Images, 62–63; Rex Features/AP Images, 65; Joe Giddens/
Press Association/AP Images, 66; Jordanian Military/Jordan TV/AP Images, 71;
Medyan Dairieh/ZumaPress/Corbis, 74–75; Red Line Editorial, 81; Olamikan Gbemiga/
AP Images, 83; Daniel Leal-Olivas/Corbis, 86–87; Tom Gianni/AP Images, 91; Khalid
Mohammed/AP Images, 93; Yves Logghe/AP Images, 94–95; Stringer/Reuters/
Corbis, 99

Editor: Mirella Miller
Series Designer: Maggie Villaume

Library of Congress Control Number: 2015944928

Cataloging-in-Publication Data

Marsico, Katie.
 ISIS / Katie Marsico.
   p. cm. -- (Special reports)
ISBN 978-1-62403-901-0 (lib. bdg.)
Includes bibliographical references and index.
1. IS (Organization)--Juvenile literature. 2. Terrorists--Iraq--Juvenile literature. 3.
Terrorists--Syria--Juvenile literature. 4. Terrorism--Religious aspects--Islam--
Juvenile literature. 5. Terrorism--Middle East--Juvenile literature.   I. Title.
956.054--dc23

2015944928

CONTENTS

CHAPTER ONE

A MENACING
MESSAGE

I n late August 2014, pictures from a haunting viral

video rapidly circulated among international media

outlets. The images the footage contained—and

the message it represented—would remain engraved

in people's minds for months to come. In the video,

US photojournalist James Foley knelt in an orange

prisoner's uniform against the backdrop of an arid

desert landscape. Foley's hands were bound behind

his back, and near him stood a man clad entirely

in black. His face shrouded in a black mask, this

mysterious captor periodically brandished a knife. As

the video unfolded, he eventually used it to behead the

40-year-old Foley.

Americans were horrified by the video released by ISIS in August 2014.

مسلمين

مي ودولة رضي بها عدد كبير من الم

JAMES FOLEY: WARTIME PHOTOJOURNALIST

Foley was born on October 18, 1973, in Rochester, New Hampshire. After graduating from Northwestern University's Medill School of Journalism in Evanston, Illinois, he decided to focus on photojournalism in war-torn areas. "I'm drawn to the drama of the conflict and the untold stories," Foley remarked during an interview with the British Broadcasting Corporation (BBC) in 2012. "But I'm drawn to the human rights side. . . . There's extreme violence, but there's also a certain sense of trying to find out who these people really are. That's the inspiring thing about it."[2] Foley initially went missing in Syria in late November 2012. He had been working for US online news company GlobalPost.

Before the photojournalist was killed, however, both he and his executioner spoke before the camera that was filming them. For his part, Foley read from a script and criticized the United States and a series of recent US air strikes carried out in Iraq. Most sources agree his captors probably forced him to make these statements. Later, the man in black—who would later be dubbed Jihadi John—issued the following warning to US president Barack Obama: "You are no longer fighting an insurgency. We are an Islamic army, and a State that has been accepted by a large number of Muslims worldwide. . . . So any attempt by you, Obama, to deny the Muslims their rights . . . will result in the bloodshed of your people."[1]

The video footage lasted less than five minutes, but it embodied an international crisis that has endured for far longer. The air strikes that are referenced—and that Foley's death was supposedly meant to atone for—were indeed carried out by US troops. They were part of a larger campaign to halt the growing power of the Islamic State in Iraq and Syria (ISIS). In response, ISIS used Foley's death as a warning of what it could and would do to answer such opposition.

A formidable and far-reaching terror organization, ISIS was not new to international security experts even before August 2014. After that date, however, people from all walks of life suddenly became more aware of the group's extremist ambitions. They also had video evidence of the brutally horrifying methods members of ISIS were willing to use to achieve them.

DWINDLING HOPE FOR SAVING A HOSTAGE

Both Foley's family and US officials had been aware of his disappearance since late 2012. At first, his parents maintained hope. They knew ISIS sometimes released hostages for ransom. The terrorist group freed other captive journalists in the spring of 2014. Then, during the summer, the US government launched a rescue mission in Syria to save Foley. Unfortunately, when US Special Forces arrived in the area where they believed Foley was being held, ISIS had already relocated him. For security reasons, they kept several details surrounding this operation shrouded in secrecy—even after the journalist's death was confirmed.

UNDERSTANDING EXTREMISM

ISIS is also frequently referred to as the Islamic State in Iraq and the Levant (ISIL or IS). The Levant is a geographic region that consists of Cyprus, Israel, Jordan, Lebanon, Syria, Palestine, and a portion of southern Turkey. While ISIS's influence was initially concentrated in Iraq and Syria, it eventually extended throughout other parts of the world as well.

The organization's main goal is to wage jihad, or holy warfare, to develop an Islamic state known as a caliphate. Islam is a religion based on the belief in a single divine being, known as Allah, and his prophet, Muhammad. Approximately 1.5 billion Muslims, or followers of Islam, practice the Islamic faith today.[3] Islam is especially common throughout South Asia, the Middle East, and Africa.

Yet not all Muslims support the agenda that organizations such as ISIS represent. ISIS is an example of a group shaped by Islamic extremism. Islamic extremists typically interpret sharia, or Islamic law, as the foundation of a global religious-political system. In such a system, a caliph, or leader, exercises total religious and political authority over his subjects' lives. Within an Islamic state, sharia and the caliph trump democracy and even human rights.

Based on these principles, members of ISIS often regard violence such as Foley's beheading as the means to a far greater end. Since forming in 2013, ISIS has claimed responsibility for numerous incidents involving kidnapping, theft, extortion, and murder. Burnings, crucifixions, and other forms of public execution are also common.

AN IMMEDIATE AND IMMENSE THREAT

As of 2015, the extent of ISIS's control was estimated to

DIFFERENT DEFINITIONS OF JIHAD

For Islamic extremist groups such as ISIS, public executions and other forms of brutality are not merely thought of as terrorism. Instead, members of these organizations regard their actions as being a necessary part of jihad. For Islamic extremists, jihad is a holy war waged by Muslims. They consider participation in jihad a sacred duty and are willing to die to defend their faith. For many Muslims, however, the term *jihad* has a separate and far less violent meaning. For individuals who do not support extremism, jihad simply refers to a personal struggle to become more devoted to Islam.

be hundreds of square miles. It stretched from Syria's coastline along the Mediterranean Sea to just south of Baghdad, the capital of Iraq. As time passes, some people fear nearby nations experiencing political unrest—such as Yemen and Libya—will also fall within ISIS's grip. Meanwhile, ISIS has managed to attract a steady stream of international recruits. These men and women come from the United States, Canada, Europe, and beyond and represent a vast array of personal and professional backgrounds.

As ISIS grows more powerful, its opponents continue to discuss how to put an end to its terrorist activities. Nations have attacked the group via air strikes. And, in Iraq

JIHADI JOHN: THE MAN BEHIND THE MASK

After the video of Foley's execution was released, intelligence officials around the world carefully studied the footage. While doing so, they painstakingly searched for any clues that would help them identify the journalist's executioner. Since he was masked, it was difficult to note many distinguishing physical features. Yet audio clips of his voice revealed he had a British accent.

Initially, the mysterious assassin was nicknamed Jihadi John. During the next several months, he appeared in additional videotaped killings committed in the name of ISIS. Then, in February 2015, US officials declared that they had obtained further information about Jihadi John's actual identity. Though not one hundred percent certain, they suspect that the man behind the mask is Mohammed Emwazi. Born in Kuwait, Emwazi moved to London, England, at a young age. Officials believe he eventually became involved in Islamic extremism and relocated to Syria in 2012.

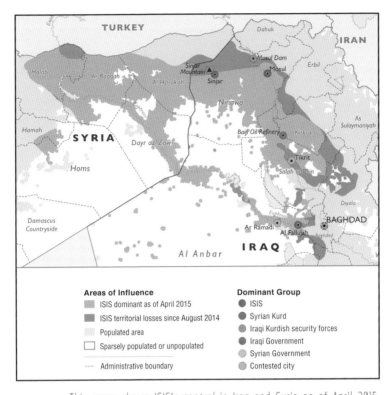

This maps shows ISIS's control in Iraq and Syria as of April 2015.

and Syria, local ground forces routinely engage in small battles with ISIS's troops.

While this mounting international conflict plays out, a long list of victims have followed in Foley's footsteps. Much like the people who support ISIS, these individuals embody a broad range of identities. From ISIS's vantage point, the crisis is about winning power over an Islamic state that knows no borders. For much of the rest of the world, however, it is about battling an immediate and undeniable threat to international security.

CHAPTER TWO

ORIGINS OF
A TERRORIST
ORGANIZATION

F oley's beheading in August 2014 earned ISIS
international attention. Yet the extremist
group evolved several years before. Most
political experts trace ISIS's origins to the terrorist
organization known as al-Qaeda, which Osama bin
Laden founded. The roots of this radical Islamic group
reach back to 1989. One of its main goals involves
"opposing non-Islamic governments with force and
violence."[1] On September 11, 2001, al-Qaeda gained
global notoriety for a series of deadly terrorist attacks
launched against the United States. These included

In the weeks following September 11, 2001, bin Laden praised the
attacks, vowing to continue fighting against the United States.

بن لادن

نظيم القاعدة

the destruction of the World Trade Center in New York City, which resulted in 2,753 deaths.[2] Initially, al-Qaeda's home base mainly extended throughout Afghanistan and Pakistan. Eventually, however, support for the group spread.

The Iraqi people were in the midst of an intense period of political instability in the early 2000s. In 2003, US troops had invaded Iraq with the goal of locating and destroying weapons of mass destruction (WMDs). They were supported by more than 40 other nations that became known as Multinational Force-Iraq or the Coalition of the Willing.[3] Members of the coalition also intended to remove Iraqi dictator Saddam Hussein from power.

Though no WMDs were ever found, US soldiers captured Hussein. But they did not begin withdrawing from the area for several years. US troops remained in Iraq to support the establishment of a democratic government. Their presence did not always succeed in promoting peace, however.

Shortly after the US invasion in 2003, bloody clashes erupted as local insurgent groups competed for power. One group was al-Qaeda in Iraq (AQI). Jordanian jihadist Abu Musab al-Zarqawi formed AQI in 2004. Within certain extremist cells, jihadists are participants who regard themselves as warriors willing to kill and die for Islam. AQI and other groups frequently relied upon radical means to battle

SADDAM HUSSEIN: INFAMOUS IRAQI DICTATOR

On July 16, 1979, Hussein assumed control of Iraq's presidency and would remain in power until 2003. Widely regarded as a dictator, Hussein earned a reputation for ruthlessly eliminating anyone he perceived as a political threat. In 1990, he attempted to take over the oil-rich nation of Kuwait. When Hussein refused to leave the area in early 1991, the United States led United Nations (UN) forces against him. Known as the Persian Gulf War, this conflict resulted in Iraqi soldiers being driven out of Kuwait by March 1991.

Hussein fell from power more than a decade later, when US troops and their allies invaded Iraq. In April 2003, he went into a period of hiding as these forces searched for WMDs—and for him. Nevertheless, Hussein was captured in December in an underground bunker. He subsequently stood trial before the new Iraqi government for "crimes against humanity."[4] After being found guilty, he was hanged in December 2006.

each other and coalition forces. It was not uncommon for them to behead hostages or carry out missions involving suicide bombers and car bombs. Tens of thousands of Iraqi civilians lost their lives.[5] Ultimately, AQI was recognized as one of the most extreme and violent of Iraq's insurgent groups.

NOT IDENTICAL TO AL-QAEDA

As time passed, it became clear AQI represented ideas that were not always identical to those of al-Qaeda. For al-Qaeda, the goal of an Islamic holy war was to battle an enemy embodied by the United States and its Western allies. The terrorist organization was confident it would one day establish a caliphate. Nevertheless, al-Qaeda's leaders did not view this step as an immediate goal.

Meanwhile, al-Zarqawi and his supporters within AQI had different ambitions. They believed in purifying the Muslim community at home. This meant violently uprooting individuals and groups whom AQI perceived as apostates, or traitors, to the purest form of Islam. AQI opposed Shiites, who represent one sect, or branch, within the Islamic faith. Shiites make up approximately

10 percent of the world's
Muslim population. In
contrast, a separate sect—the
Sunnis—represent as much
as 90 percent.[6] Compared
to Shiites, Sunnis typically
consider themselves to be more
orthodox, or traditional, in their
religious practices and beliefs.

From the perspective of
AQI, however, Shiites were not
merely less traditional Muslims.
They were a threat to the
establishment of a caliphate,
which al-Zarqawi saw as an
imminent goal. Members of AQI therefore did not hesitate
to viciously attack Shiites or even other jihadists who failed
to share their exact ideologies.

The differences between al-Qaeda and AQI gradually
grew more apparent. In the summer of 2006, al-Zarqawi
died as the result of a US air strike. In October, his
successor, Abu Ayyub al-Masri, founded the Islamic State

SUNNIS VERSUS SHIITES

One of the main divisions between
Sunnis and Shiites traces back
to their differing beliefs following
Muhammad's death in 632 CE.
The Sunnis decided to follow
the prophet's adviser—Abu Bakr.
Meanwhile, the Shiites looked
to Muhammad's cousin and
son-in-law Ali as their new caliph.
Centuries later, they still believe
only Ali's heirs can rightfully lead
the caliphate.

Sunnis tend to form the
majority of the Muslim population
in most nations where Islam is
practiced. Exceptions to this rule
are Iran, Iraq, Bahrain, Azerbaijan,
and Yemen, where most Muslims
are Shiite. Today, religious violence
between Sunnis and Shiites
often shapes civil wars and other
conflicts that occur throughout
the Middle East.

Iraqi soldiers raise their weapons, ready to defend their territory against ISIS.

in Iraq (ISI). He declared fellow-extremist Abu Omar al-Baghdadi to be its leader. ISI maintained ties with al-Qaeda but had a unique identity. Unlike al-Qaeda's core values, religious violence and an urgent pressure to build a caliphate defined the new group's backbone.

For a while, insurgent organizations such as ISI appeared to lose the upper hand to coalition forces. They also faced opposition from Muslim fighters who participated in what was known as the Sunni Awakening Movement. Members of the Awakening received training

MORE TO THE
STORY

THE SUNNI AWAKENING MOVEMENT

During the Sunni Awakening Movement, the US and Iraqi governments backed various Sunni tribes who united to fight insurgents. According to most experts, the Awakening started in 2006. In many cases, Sunni participants joined forces with former Iraqi military officials. Together, they organized a militia that served several purposes.

For members of the Awakening, one immediate goal was to patrol areas groups such as AQI were known to control. Sunni fighters were therefore credited with restoring safety and security to their communities. Yet Iraqis who joined the Awakening had other motives, as well. Specifically, most hoped to regain a measure of power in Iraq's primarily Shiite government.

The Congressional Research Service estimated Awakening forces to number close to 100,000 individuals.[7] Though the United States was helping fund their salaries, some US officials expressed concern that such efforts could backfire. If Iraq and the United States ultimately withdrew their support, these Sunnis would lose their paid positions.

As the United States prepared to leave Iraq, US officials pushed for fighters to be formally incorporated into national security forces. Yet by 2011, only a fraction of the Sunnis were granted either military or government jobs. For those who did not transition into these roles, disappointment sometimes drove them to align with ISIS. Others were arrested or executed by Iraq's primarily Shiite government.

and support from the US and Iraqi governments as part of a larger attempt to weaken insurgents. In 2010, both al-Masri and al-Baghdadi were killed fighting these forces. Yet the terrorist group they had played a role in creating was far from finished. In fact, it was already gaining a deadly momentum.

SPREADING TERROR IN A SECURITY VACUUM

By 2009, the United States and its partners within the coalition had started withdrawing from Iraq. They departed after spending nearly six years trying to help the Iraqis cultivate a democracy following a long period of dictatorship. As many insurgents realized, this removal of troops left Iraq's new government in a vulnerable position. As foreign troops went home, it was far more difficult for Iraqi officials to address unrest and maintain national security. In addition, Iraq's primarily Shiite government remained at odds with the country's Sunni population. For Iraqi cleric Abu Bakr al-Baghdadi, the moment was therefore right for ISI to gain a stronger foothold. A special council within ISI had appointed al-Baghdadi leader of

ISI leader al-Baghdadi presents a sermon at a mosque in Iraq.

the group in April 2010. Before that, he had served time

in Camp Bucca as a result of his suspected involvement

with AQI.

Camp Bucca—a US-run prison located near the

Iraq-Kuwait border—closed in 2009. Prior to that point,

roughly 100,000 detainees had passed through its

gates during a six-year period.[8] A large number of these

individuals had already had significant exposure to

violence and extremism before passing through Camp

Bucca's gates. Some had formerly been loyal to Hussein,

and others were Islamic jihadists who had been involved

in terrorist activities. Life at the detention center allowed men from both groups to collaborate and intensify their radicalism. Military veteran Andrew Thompson and academic Jeremi Suri observed:

> Before their detention, Mr. al-Baghdadi and others were violent radicals, intent on attacking America. Their time in prison deepened their extremism and gave them opportunities to broaden their following. . . . The prisons became virtual terrorist universities: The hardened radicals were the professors, the other detainees were the students, and the prison authorities played the role of absent custodian.[9]

Within Camp Bucca, al-Baghdadi was respected and regarded as a leader by fellow inmates. This perception of him continued among extremists once he was released and became head of ISI. In the early years of his regime, the organization experienced a revival in a nation frequently dubbed a "security vacuum."[10] This description was applied to Iraq in 2011, when the United States completed its withdrawal of troops. The foreign military presence that had previously supported the development of a more democratic Iraqi government was gone. In turn, the resulting lack of security made Iraq even more vulnerable to political instability.

WARNING
تحذير

No photograph[y or videota]
ممنوع التصوير
camera equ[ipment and i]
مصادرة جميع أجهزة التصوير
will be [confiscated]

BASIC RIGHTS [UNDER THE G]C.
CONVENTION
حقوق الأساسية في معاهدة جنيف
1.To be tr[e]ated humanely.
المعاملة الإنسانية.
2.Visitation [b]y family membe[r]
زيارة الأسرة
العائلة
3.Fulfillment [o]f religious pract[ice]
حرية ممارسة الطقوس الدينية.
4.Free from hu[m]iliation or haras[s]
عدم الإذلال أو المضايقة بدون سبب.
5.Access to [G]eneva Conventi[on]
إمكانية الحصول على بنود معاهدة جنيف.

Camp Bucca was the largest US prison camp in Iraq before it closed
in 2009.

Members of ISI took advantage of this situation and kept up a steady stream of terrorist attacks. In their efforts to create a pure and powerful Islamic state, they launched Operation Breaking the Walls. This initiative lasted from July 2012 to July 2013. Its focus was planning and carrying out prison breaks to free political extremists. Amidst gunfire and explosions, hundreds of detainees escaped from various detention centers throughout Iraq. According to US officials, a few hundred joined ISI's ranks. Yet not all of these men remained in Iraq. Some fled across the border to Syria and supported what would soon become ISI's expansion into that nation.

CHAPTER THREE

NEW AND UNDENIABLY DANGEROUS

F or members of ISI, establishing a caliphate ultimately involved more than merely purifying the Muslim community. While overpowering a near enemy was critical to their cause, they also recognized it was important to expand and grow. This meant gaining control of territory in other countries, including Syria, one of Iraq's neighbors to the west.

In 2011, al-Baghdadi began taking steps to organize Syrian jihadist groups. For this reason, he dispatched one of his agents, Abu Muhammad al-Jawlani, across the border. Soon, al-Jawlani headed

Al-Nusra quickly gained traction in Syria and spread from territory to territory using tactics similar to ISI.

ABU BAKR AL-BAGHDADI: ELUSIVE LEADER

Much of al-Baghdadi's life and day-to-day whereabouts remain shrouded in mystery. This is largely due to security concerns, since he is at constant risk of being tracked down by ISIS's enemies. Al-Baghdadi was probably born in Samarra, Iraq, in 1971. It is likely he was serving as an Islamic religious leader when US forces invaded Iraq in 2003.

Experts offer differing opinions on how al-Baghdadi evolved into a violent extremist. According to some accounts, he already had radical beliefs prior to his imprisonment at Camp Bucca. Yet other reports claim al-Baghdadi's time there was what shaped his violent jihadist views. After establishing himself as ISIS's leader, he became known as a ruthless commander. According to most sources, al-Baghdadi is also exceptionally organized and demonstrates a keen sense of military strategy.

a rebel organization known as the al-Nusra Front that was identified as having ties to al-Qaeda.

Al-Nusra quickly became well-known throughout Syria as a highly effective fighting force. Much like ISI, it gained strength during a period of national turmoil. Starting in 2011, civil war divided the Syrian people. Various rebel groups rose up to protest a government headed by President Bashar al-Assad. These rebel groups objected to the poverty and lack of rights many citizens experienced during al-Assad's dictatorship. Inevitably, a large number of rebels therefore primarily focused on creating political changes.

While al-Nusra shared this goal of protesting al-Assad, it was also determined to set up an Islamic state in Syria. Yet al-Jawlani was not necessarily interested in stretching his authority beyond Syrian borders. Meanwhile, al-Baghdadi was eager to control Iraq, Syria, and territory he hoped would one day reach far beyond those two nations. Within a few years, the differences between al-Baghdadi's ambitions and those of al-Jawlani proved a mounting source of tension.

ABSORBING AL-NUSRA

In April 2013, al-Baghdadi declared that ISI was officially absorbing al-Nusra. He said the

SYRIA: A WAR-WEARY NATION

As of March 2015, Syria's civil war had resulted in an estimated 200,000 Syrian casualties. Approximately 11 million other people were forced to flee their homes as violence and chaos engulfed their communities.[1] Along the way, both Syria's government and various rebel forces have been accused of a wide range of war crimes. These include kidnapping, rape, torture, and murder.

In August 2013, multiple areas around Damascus, Syria, were ravaged by chemical warfare. Across the world, people expressed a combination of shock and horror at images associated with these attacks. Pictures and video footage of men, women, and children dealing with the effects of nerve gas quickly spread on the Internet. Both President al-Assad's regime and rebel groups blamed each other for the devastation.

Such activities also led to Syria becoming the focal point of an ongoing humanitarian crisis. International media outlets have chronicled the suffering of refugees attempting to escape local conflict. In addition to being displaced from their homes, many of these individuals struggle with hunger, poverty, and disease.

merging of the two groups marked the birth of the Islamic State in Iraq and al-Sham (ISIS). The term "al-Sham" refers to the region encompassed by Syria. Al-Jawlani rejected al-Baghdadi's plans for al-Nusra. He was supported by Ayman al-Zawahiri—the leader of al-Qaeda. Both men argued that al-Nusra was an independent branch of al-Qaeda and was therefore not subject to al-Baghdadi's demands. Just as important, not everyone within either al-Qaeda or al-Nusra shared all of ISI's ideologies and ambitions. Yet, despite the objections of al-Jawlani and al-Zawahiri, al-Baghdadi refused to back down.

"[ISIS] will remain, as long as we have a vein pumping or an eye blinking," al-Baghdadi asserted. "It remains, and we will not compromise nor give it up . . . until we die."[2] Unwilling to bend, he led ISIS in what eventually evolved into a heated conflict with al-Nusra. Some troops left al-Nusra to fight for al-Baghdadi. Still others maintained their loyalty to al-Jawlani and al-Qaeda.

By March 2014, violence between the terrorist groups had resulted in approximately 3,000 deaths.[3] By the summer, ISIS militants had managed to seize control of oil fields in eastern Syria. This was an undeniable blow

Al-Nusra fighters wanted to keep their independence from ISIS and al-Baghdadi.

to al-Nusra, which had relied upon the fields to fund its efforts.

After observing the hostilities that had erupted throughout Syria—and witnessing al-Baghdadi's unwillingness to yield—al-Qaeda severed ties with ISIS. Al-Baghdadi had been leading his group down a separate path for some time. Beginning in 2014, however, al-Zawahiri officially renounced any association with al-Baghdadi's legion of jihadists. From his perspective, they were too volatile and brutal toward other Muslims. As for al-Nusra, it entered into an unpredictable and often inconsistent relationship with ISIS. Even after 2013, the

WHY ABANDON AL-QAEDA?

Before ISIS became an internationally feared threat, al-Qaeda was arguably the world's most infamous terrorist organization. Under al-Zawahiri's leadership, however, some people believed al-Qaeda's influence had begun dwindling. According to certain terrorism experts, ISIS represented a newer, more vibrant jihadist force. "For the last ten years or more, [al-Zawahiri] . . . hasn't really done very much more than issue a few statements and videos," said Richard Barrett in June 2014. Barrett once worked as a counterterrorism chief for the United Kingdom's foreign intelligence service. "Whereas al-Baghdadi . . . has captured cities . . . has mobilized huge amounts of people . . . [and] is killing ruthlessly throughout Iraq and Syria. If you were a guy who wanted action, you would go with Baghdadi."[5]

two organizations continued clashing violently. In certain situations, however, they also supported each other on the battlefield.

Beginning in 2014, ISIS successfully started growing within Syria's borders. In the months ahead, it managed to force at least one-third of Syria under its control. According to one former ISIS militant, this was all part of a much larger plan for a vast and powerful caliphate. "The main and principal goal of [ISIS] that they tell their new members is to establish an Islamic state that will encompass the Arab world," the ex-fighter remarked. "And, after that, we go to other countries."[4]

THE TAKEOVER OF MOSUL AND TIKRIT

In order to build a sprawling caliphate, members of ISIS forcefully seized several key cities throughout Iraq and Syria. By June 2014, they were already in control of Fallujah and portions of Ramadi, Baiji, and the Kirkuk Province in Iraq. They had also captured a handful of Syrian border towns.

Then, on June 9, ISIS extremists began a two-day siege in Mosul, Iraq's second-largest city. During their rampage, militants took over the local airport, television stations, and the governor's office. In response, nearly half a million people fled Mosul.[6]

ANALYZING ISIS'S FLAG

One of the common images associated with ISIS is a black flag that features white Arabic lettering. It is also often referred to as the "black standard" or "black banner." The writing on the upper portion of the flag states, "There is no god but God, Muhammad is the messenger of God." In Islam, this phrase is called the *shahada* and is regarded as a declaration of faith. The text in the white circle in the middle of the flag repeats the statement, "Muhammad is the messenger of God."[7] The shahada is actually part of several flags flown throughout Islamic nations. As a result, many Muslims object to how ISIS militants have used it to represent their terrorist agenda.

"CONTINUE YOUR MARCH AS THE BATTLE IS NOT YET RAGING. . . . DON'T GIVE UP A HAND'S WIDTH OF GROUND YOU'VE LIBERATED."[8]

—ISIS SPOKESMAN ABU MOHAMMED AL-ADNANI SPEAKING TO ISIS FIGHTERS IN IRAQ

In addition, several police and military officers abandoned their posts as ISIS approached.

Two days later, ISIS had also invaded Hussein's hometown of Tikrit, Iraq. Again, both civilians and local authorities attempted to escape the city as ISIS's fighters poured over its borders. Often wearing black masks, the armed militants appeared to target security forces affiliated with the Iraqi government. They set fire to a police station and other buildings. They also pulled terrified, confused people from their cars at checkpoints and shot them on the spot. In addressing such violence, Iraqi officials vowed revenge. "We are not going to allow this to carry on, regardless of the price," announced Iraqi

ISIS'S ADVANCES

As of the summer of 2014, ISIS was already in control of multiple towns and cities in northern Iraq. It had started expanding into northern and eastern Syria as well. For the terrorist group, such expansion was an important part of its core ideology. ISIS was intent on building a vast caliphate, which, from the perspective of the militants, required an aggressive approach. The organization's reputation for being swift and ruthless generally worked to its advantage, too. It was not unusual for security forces in Syria and other countries to abandon their posts and attempt to flee when confronted by ISIS. This made it easier for militants to take over populated regions. It also provided them with greater opportunities to gather weapons and supplies. Along the way, ISIS gained access to valuable resources such as dams and oil fields.

ISIS militants destroy ancient religious artifacts, such as statues and art, in a Mosul museum during their takeover of the city in June 2014.

Prime Minister Nouri Maliki.[9] Yet the violence and chaos that played out in Mosul and Tikrit echoed far beyond the Middle East. Within a matter of days, ISIS's swift and successful displays of aggression made headlines across the globe.

"The speed of the jihadis' advance has shocked the Iraqi government and its Western allies," a reporter for the BBC noted.[10] Indeed, much of the world suddenly became more aware of the organization that had begun as an al-Qaeda splinter group. And based on what people had witnessed by the summer of 2014, ISIS posed a serious and significant international threat.

"[ISIS IS] BEYOND JUST A TERRORIST GROUP. . . . THEY MARRY IDEOLOGY [AND] A SOPHISTICATION OF STRATEGIC AND TACTICAL MILITARY PROWESS. THIS IS BEYOND ANYTHING WE HAVE SEEN, AND WE MUST PREPARE FOR EVERYTHING."[11]

—US DEFENSE SECRETARY CHUCK HAGEL

An ISIS fighter proudly displays the flag as militants continue to violently move through the Middle East.

CHAPTER FOUR

LASTING
IMPACTS

T he advance of ISIS did not stop in the Iraqi towns of Mosul and Tikrit. By late June 2014, militants fighting for the terrorist organization overran large stretches of territory north of Baghdad. Yet ISIS did more than establish geographic boundaries as its power grew throughout the Middle East. It forever changed the existences of countless local people from all walks of life. Extremists did not merely target government officials and security forces. In many cases, they threatened, persecuted, and killed ordinary civilians.

Sometimes militants initially attempted to reassure residents of cities and villages that they seized throughout Iraq and Syria. In Mosul, for example, they told local citizens that they "[were] not in danger . . . and

ISIS took control of various crossing points along the Iraq–Syria border as it gathered more power.

should go back to work."[1] Nevertheless, not everyone in Mosul—or any other area overpowered by ISIS—found it easy to take such words to heart. By the summer of 2014, rumors of the group's brutal tactics were widespread. In most cases, people who encountered ISIS faced three possible fates—accept its ideologies, pay a fine, or face death.

IMPOSSIBLE ULTIMATUMS

Despite their initial promises, ISIS jihadists quickly proved themselves unwilling to accept ideas or behavior that they perceived as a challenge. Along the way, several ethnic and religious groups became their targets. These included Kurdish religious minorities such as the Yazidis. The Kurdish people are members of the fourth-largest ethnic group in the Middle East. Between 25 million and 35 million Kurds inhabit a mountainous region that stretches across portions of Turkey, Iraq, Syria, Iran, and Armenia.[2] The Yazidis make up a portion of this population and practice a religion based on elements of various faiths. Christians, Shiites, and Turkic-speaking peoples are examples of additional groups that have been threatened by ISIS.

Once militants began occupying Iraq and Syria, they often tried to force their beliefs upon local residents. For example, in the spring of 2014, members of ISIS that were operating within Syria kidnapped 140 Kurdish schoolboys. Jihadists in armed pickup trucks forced the students off their school buses. According to a handful of boys who managed to later escape, the period ahead was shaped by terror and attempted brainwashing. One escapee eventually recalled the threat that militants made to them early on in their captivity. "'If you try to leave,' [they] said, 'we will cut your heads off.'"[3]

THE YAZIDIS: A PERSECUTED PEOPLE

According to some historians, the Yazidi religion dates back to the 1100s. It began with a community in what is now Kurdistan and is rooted in a mixture of faiths. The Yazidis's beliefs are partially influenced by Islam, Christianity, and Judaism. They are also shaped by an ancient Persian religion called Zoroastrianism and an Eastern Mediterranean religion known as Mithraism.

The Yazidi faith features one God but is more heavily focused on an angel named Tawusî Melek. This angel is a defiant figure who acts as a type of middleman between God and humans. But to some Muslims outside the Yazidi religion, Tawusî Melek is a devil-like being. As a result, the Yazidis have faced misunderstanding, persecution, and accusations of devil worship since the late 1800s. Many members of this faith claim their religious history includes multiple genocides. For the Yazidis, their plight at the hands of ISIS therefore represents one of numerous attempts to destroy them.

"YOU GO INTO AYAN AL-ARAB [IN NORTHERN SYRIA], AND THERE ARE NO YOUTHS. ALL MY FRIENDS ARE TAKEN. I FEEL I CANNOT SMILE. MY WHOLE LIFE AND ALL MY DAYS WERE WITH MY CLASSMATES, AND NOW THERE IS NOTHING."[5]

—KURDISH SCHOOLBOY WHO ESCAPED ISIS MILITANTS

In the days that followed, members of ISIS schooled the boys in sharia law and their notions of jihad. Part of their education involved watching videos of executions and suicide missions. Even after escaping ISIS, those students who fled feared for their safety. They worried they might face execution if they were ever recaptured.

As ISIS militants continued expanding their caliphate, countless other people in their path dealt with similar threats. In Mosul, for example, jihadists presented Christians with the following ultimatum—convert to Islam, pay a large fine, or accept "death by the sword."[4] In many situations, members of targeted groups perished as ISIS seized control of larger portions of Iraq and Syria. Militants were known to hang, behead, or crucify such individuals.

People who were not killed struggled to survive in a world where their communities were routinely rocked by rape, abduction, torture, and bombings. For many, day-to-day life was heavily influenced by activities that witnesses likened to genocide and "crimes against humanity."[6]

Within this climate of violence, no one seemed immune to ISIS's advance—including women and children. When the terrorist organization took female prisoners, it frequently sold them as slaves or forced them into arranged marriages with militants. One 15-year-old Yazidi girl recalled the day she was abducted by ISIS extremists in northern Iraq. "I was crying and grabbing my mother's hand," she recollected. "One of the Islamic State members came and beat me and put a pistol to my head. My mother said I should go so I wouldn't be killed."[7] Eventually, the enslaved girl made a daring escape and was able to return to her family. Yet she still has not been reunited with her

NO CERTAINTY OF SURVIVAL

As many Christians living in Mosul discovered, converting to Islam did not guarantee their safety once ISIS invaded. Initially, militants marked the homes of all Christian residents with the Arabic letter *N*. This marking stood for *Nasara*, which is an early Islamic word meaning "Christian."

In one case, a man who initially refused to convert to Islam explained that ISIS first took his money. Later, they kidnapped his wife and children. At last, he accepted Islam as his religion and was reunited with his family. Not long afterward, however, the former Christian said that militants began hinting at the possibility of marrying off his ten-year-old daughter. According to these militants, his child was not too young to be a bride, based on sharia law. The man and his family became refugees and fled. Their situation was not unique within ISIS-controlled territories.

sisters, who were seized under similar circumstances. As of the autumn of 2014, ISIS had abducted an estimated 5,000 to 7,000 Yazidis.[8] The jihadists responsible for such kidnappings argued that sharia law justified their enslavement of certain groups.

If anyone living in the areas ISIS invaded disagreed with the group's ultimatums, they took a considerable risk in doing so. In order to reinforce their reputation for iron-fisted authority, militants purposely intimidated residents of the cities and villages they overran. During the summer of 2014, reports circulated of jihadists planting their victims' heads on spikes in local parks. Knowing that ISIS was capable of such brutality, people frequently fled their homes.

SOLD INTO SLAVERY

From the perspective of ISIS fighters, it was not immoral to enslave female members of the groups they persecuted. Due to their religious or ethnic differences, these girls and women were often viewed as infidels. In some cases, militants kidnapped and sold abductees as young as eight years old.

In August 2014, residents of the village of Kuchu, Iraq, experienced such brutality firsthand. After rounding up local men to be shot, ISIS jihadists gathered together the girls and women to be auctioned off. A teenager named Farida was among this group. After escaping slavery, she described her brutal treatment at the hands of various masters. If Farida showed any type of disobedience, she was locked up, beaten, or starved. She also endured repeated rapes and attempted to take her own life numerous times. "We said, 'We are human beings,'" Farida recalled when discussing a plea she and other enslaved girls made to ISIS militants. "They said, 'You are our property. . . . You are infidels. We will do what we want with you.'"[9]

HARSH REALITIES FOR REFUGEES

As ISIS gained power in Iraq and Syria, millions of refugees sought to relocate. Yet the challenge of moving and beginning a new life in another region or country often proved extremely difficult. For starters, several areas were already experiencing the strain of accepting refugees that predated ISIS.

Years of fighting in both Iraq and Syria had driven many residents from their original communities. When ISIS's progress fueled a new wave of refugees, regions such

"FOOD, CLOTHES, MEDICINES, IMPORTANT PAPERS—EVERYTHING WE LEFT BEHIND. I DON'T KNOW HOW WE'LL GET BY. SOMEONE DONATED THOSE BLANKETS AND PILLOWS, AND THAT'S ALL WE HAVE."[10]

—CHRISTIAN REFUGEE LIVING ON THE OUTSKIRTS OF IRBIL, IRAQ

A refugee camp on the Turkey-Syria border is filled with Kurds escaping from the violence and persecution of ISIS.

as Iraqi Kurdistan swelled beyond capacity in 2014. The streets grew more congested, and resources such as water and electricity became scarce.

Without enough suitable housing to accommodate refugees, these displaced populations were typically forced to set up makeshift camps. Within these camps, hunger, exposure to the weather, and sanitary issues created a multitude of health problems. In addition, children suffered from a lack of education and overall stability. Still, when choosing between the challenges of a refugee camp and persecution by ISIS, most people preferred the former option.

In many situations, however, relocation was no easy task. For example, on June 28, 2014, Kurdish officials responded to the growing humanitarian crisis in Iraqi Kurdistan by limiting the number of refugees allowed to pass through border crossings. In many other cases, refugees had little time to put much thought into selecting a new destination. They simply needed to flee as soon as possible. This was the case in August 2014, when ISIS stormed the town of Sinjar, Iraq. One college student described the chaos and panic that characterized his

MORE TO THE
STORY

LIFE ON THE RUN FROM ISIS

For the refugees who fled ISIS in 2014, escaping advancing militants was often only the start of an ongoing battle for survival. Most of these individuals considered themselves fortunate to evade the terrorist group. Nevertheless, the new life that awaited them beyond ISIS's grasp was typically filled with uncertainty and suffering.

"We have no electricity or running water, and we have not washed in days," remarked one refugee living along the Iraq–Turkey border. "But at least we are safe from [ISIS]." Some of the men, women, and children running from ISIS militants settled in abandoned buildings. Others dwelled in outdoor camps where tents served as the main form of shelter. In either instance, scorching summer heat, frigid winter weather, and periodic rainstorms posed serious challenges.

"The situation for the children is worse," noted one Yazidi mother. "When they get up in the morning, their tiny bodies are so stiff from the cold, they can't move. We have no proper clothing for them."[1] Limited food, clean water, electricity, and medical supplies created additional problems. The jihadists' continued progress throughout the Middle East also sparked a terrifying sense of instability. For refugees, any temporary relief from the horrors of ISIS was therefore filled with few guarantees—and almost constant hardships.

family's departure: "There were a . . . thousand cars, and my father drove a car for six hours—Three hours in the dust and three hours on the road. When we were in the dust, we couldn't see anything, just cars running away. We didn't know where we were going."[12]

To avoid ISIS militants, large numbers of Yazidis who had been residing in Sinjar fled into the nearby Sinjar Mountains. Approximately 40,000 of these individuals quickly found themselves trapped in an impossible situation. On the one hand, ISIS militants swarmed near Mount Sinjar's base—ready to attack anyone who descended. At the same time, the Yazidi refugees began suffering from a severe water shortage. Either way, they appeared likely to become the victims of a mass genocide.

"There is a collective attempt to exterminate the Yazidi people," observed Iraqi lawmaker Vian Dakhil.[13] Dakhil issued her plea to fellow legislators in Iraq. Yet officials in other countries heard it as well. The world was already aware of ISIS and the numerous threats it represented. Soon, however, global forces would take a stronger and more united stand against the terrorist organization.

A Yazidi family sits outside their makeshift home atop Mount Sinjar.

CHAPTER FIVE

EARLY
RESPONSES

T he plight of the Yazidis was but one humanitarian crisis created by ISIS. For several months, the international community had been monitoring reports of the organization's military activities and persecution of various religious and ethnic groups. During the summer of 2014, ISIS had continued storming throughout Iraq and Syria, seizing oil fields, military airports, and army bases.

The militants' ability to win territory and resources proved it was more than a short-lived and insignificant al-Qaeda splinter group. Then, in June 2014, ISIS announced that its formation of a caliphate had effectively erased all state borders. In other words, al-Baghdadi declared that his authority extended over

An oil refinery burns in the distance as the Iraqi army and ISIS fight for control of the oil throughout the country.

the world's roughly 1.5 billion Muslim citizens, regardless of where they lived. For this reason, al-Baghdadi's followers also began simply calling their group the Islamic State (IS). Yet many people still referred to them using the acronym they were most familiar with—ISIS.

As ISIS revealed its brutality and strength, humanitarian organizations and world leaders alike prepared to more actively address its increasing power. On June 30, 2014, the US Department of Defense (DOD) indicated the United States was dispatching 300 troops to Iraq.[1] Officials explained this decision was partially designed to support the Iraqi government in its battle against the jihadists. In addition, they hoped to secure the US embassy and airport in Baghdad.

At the time, the US military presence was regarded as more of a safeguard than an attack force. Nevertheless, President Obama emphasized this status could potentially change, saying, "The United States would be prepared to take targeted military action in Iraq if and when . . . the situation required it."[2]

Obama delivers a speech explaining the use of US troops in Iraq.

In the months that followed, Obama and other world leaders decided the situation did call for a more aggressive approach. For starters, ISIS jihadists were steadily moving closer to areas where US military and diplomatic personnel were stationed. The group's advance throughout Iraq therefore posed a direct threat to the safety of these individuals. In addition, by August, the Yazidis flight to the Sinjar Mountains signaled how ISIS's persecution could rapidly lead to genocide.

AIR STRIKES AND HUMANITARIAN EFFORTS

On August 7, 2014, President Obama delivered a televised address. During this speech, he informed viewers the United States would be launching targeted air strikes against ISIS in Iraq. He also stated he had authorized US humanitarian efforts designed to aid the Yazidis stranded atop Mount Sinjar.

Obama offered assurances he had no intention of committing ground troops to a new war in Iraq. On the other hand, he believed it was essential to help the Iraqis overpower terrorist groups such as ISIS. He hoped to accomplish this goal by supporting their development of a stronger, more stable government. In the meantime, however, Obama stated military action was needed to defend both persecuted refugees and US citizens in Iraq.

The United States launched its first wave of air strikes against ISIS on August 8. A combination of drones and fighter jets were used to bomb the militants' artillery and convoy units. US forces targeted northern Iraq, where the extremists were continually moving closer to Irbil. Just one day later, the Iraqi air force directed additional rounds of air strikes against ISIS militants in Sinjar. These maneuvers were designed to disrupt their continued attacks against the Yazidis.

NOT COMMITTING TO GROUND COMBAT

In 2011, the United States withdrew the final wave of ground troops from Iraq following its 2003 invasion. In the years ahead, many US citizens were hesitant to become involved in another war there. Some expressed doubt that storming into Iraq in 2003 had accomplished much good in the first place.

Critics of this 2003 military operation pointed to the fact that no WMDs had ever been located. In addition, though Hussein had been removed from power, the Iraqi government remained unstable more than ten years later. So, by 2014, the idea of committing more US lives to conflict in Iraq was not necessarily popular. As a result, Obama sought to reassure the public once air strikes against ISIS were underway. "As your commander in chief, I will not commit you and the rest of our armed forces to fighting another ground war in Iraq," the president stated. "After a decade of massive ground deployments, it is more effective to use our unique capabilities in support of partners on the ground so they can secure their own countries' futures. And that is the only solution that will succeed over the long term."[3]

Meanwhile, US planes started airdropping desperately needed supplies to refugees trapped in the Sinjar Mountains. They were joined in their efforts by nations such as Australia, Canada, and France. In most cases, pilots making the drops had to be escorted by fighter planes. This precaution helped offer protection against any surface-to-air attacks attempted by ISIS. With the help of Iraqi forces, aircraft also began transporting refugees off Mount Sinjar.

Initially, the involvement of outside countries in the struggle against ISIS seemed like a turning point. As a result of air strikes, Kurdish and Iraqi troops started recapturing lost territory. At long last, ISIS's progress appeared to be slowed. Within months, efforts to oppose the terrorist organization intensified. Specifically, a growing list of nations joined a task force that was ultimately dubbed Operation Inherent Resolve. One of the major goals of this operation was to carry out additional targeted air strikes within Iraq and Syria in order to defeat

> "WE ARE A PEACEFUL PEOPLE. WE DO NOT SEEK OUT CONFRONTATION. BUT WE NEED TO UNDERSTAND. WE CANNOT IGNORE THIS THREAT TO OUR SECURITY AND THAT OF OUR ALLIES."[4]
>
> —BRITISH PRIME MINISTER DAVID CAMERON

ISIS. Eventually, 62 international participants united to take a stand against the militants. By early 2015, they included Australia, Bahrain, Belgium, Canada, Denmark, France, Jordan, the Netherlands, Saudi Arabia, the United Arab Emirates, the United Kingdom, and the United States.

Not every country involved in Operation Inherent Resolve was directly responsible for conducting air strikes. Yet each contributed to initiatives that opposed ISIS. Some nations supplied military aid, advisers, and training to Kurdish, Iraqi, and Syrian troops. Others worked closely with humanitarian organizations such as the United Nations (UN) to help refugees.

THE UN: GLOBAL OPPOSITION TO ISIS

The UN was among the global organizations that responded to the growing problems created by ISIS in Syria and Iraq. World leaders founded the UN in 1945 to help promote peace and protect international human rights. The group was formed to address several humanitarian crises that arose following World War II (1939–1945).

The UN featured 193 member states in 2015. Delegates from these nations meet to discuss and act upon multiple issues, including threats posed by terrorist organizations such as ISIS. In August 2014, the UN passed a resolution formally condemning militants' abuse of human rights. In addition, they established sanctions to punish nations that provided support to ISIS. Moving forward, the UN also organized humanitarian aid efforts to assist individuals being victimized by the group.

FROM THE
HEADLINES

DARING MISSIONS
ATOP MOUNT SINJAR

Aiding the Yazidis trapped on Mount Sinjar was both complex and dangerous. Any aircraft dropping aid to the refugees was at risk of being fired upon by ISIS. Secondly, the drops often resulted in desperate men, women, and children attempting to climb aboard the planes. When space allowed, these individuals were frequently flown to more stable locations.

On August 11, 2014, a US news crew accompanied Iraqi and Kurdish forces as they delivered supplies to Mount Sinjar. Ultimately, the plane also transported roughly 20 refugees off the mountain. CNN reporter Ivan Watson described how the harrowing rescue mission played out: "We landed on several short occasions, and that's where—amid this explosion of dust and chaos—these desperate civilians came racing towards the helicopter, throwing their children on board the aircraft. The crew was just trying to pull up as many people as possible. . . . They flew in shooting; they flew out shooting."[5]

An Iraqi Air Force helicopter makes a daring landing to drop supplies for the refugees on Mount Sinjar.

INVOLVEMENT IN OPERATION INHERENT RESOLVE

According to US military officials, the name Operation Inherent Resolve was "intended to reflect the unwavering resolve and deep commitment of the US and partner nations . . . around the globe to eliminate the terrorist group [ISIS] and the threat they pose to . . . the . . . international community." As of early 2015, the complete list of participants in Operation Inherent Resolve included 62 countries.[7]

[THE UN] DEPLORES AND CONDEMNS IN THE STRONGEST TERMS THE TERRORIST ACTS OF [ISIS] AND ITS VIOLENT EXTREMIST IDEOLOGY, AND ITS CONTINUED GROSS, SYSTEMATIC AND WIDESPREAD ABUSES OF HUMAN RIGHTS AND VIOLATIONS OF INTERNATIONAL HUMANITARIAN LAW."[8]

—UN RESOLUTION 2170

IMPACTS OF INTERNATIONAL INVOLVEMENT

Beginning in August 2014, the international struggle to overcome ISIS gained momentum. Early on, however, US officials and military experts were cautious in expressing their optimism. It was true air strikes had briefly interrupted the militants' establishment of a far-reaching caliphate. And within five months, US officials announced thousands of ISIS fighters had perished in combat since the previous summer.[6]

Nevertheless, terrorism experts estimated the group could rally more than five times that amount of jihadists. In August 2014, Obama accurately predicted that defeating ISIS would be a "long-term project." He also described the organization as an "aggressive adversary" and acknowledged that US officials had initially underestimated ISIS's strength. "There is no doubt that their advance . . . over the past several months has been more rapid than the intelligence estimates and the expectations of policymakers," the president stated.[9]

Obama's military officials offered similar opinions not long after the first air strikes occurred. "Our current operations are limited in scope," remarked Lieutenant General William Mayville Jr., the director of operations for

Syrian Kurd refugees receive food at a refugee camp in Suruc, Turkey.

MORE TO THE STORY

A RANGE OF REACTIONS TO AIR STRIKES

In September 2014, the United States decided to launch air strikes against ISIS in Syria. Bahrain, Jordan, Saudi Arabia, the United Arab Emirates, and Qatar joined US forces in their efforts. US involvement inspired a wide range of reactions from international voices. These opinions made headlines and, in many cases, were deeply influenced by the complicating factor of Syria's ongoing civil war.

Some nations such as the United Kingdom expressed their firm support of US military action within Syria's borders. So did various Syrian rebels who stood in opposition to the dictatorship that ruled their country.

President al-Assad and his officials implied that if such attacks ended up disrupting their seat of power, then they were against the law. Russia, which had proven itself friendly toward al-Assad's government, also condemned the bombings.

Meanwhile, Muslim and Arab groups in the United States voiced doubts as to the long-term success of the air strikes. Some condemned US officials for not having stepped in earlier—not just to defeat ISIS, but to aid Syrians who opposed al-Assad.

"I believe US policy remains shortsighted," said Salam al-Marayati, head of the Muslim Public Affairs Council. "It only manages the symptoms of violent extremism. It doesn't deal with the root causes. Unfortunately, I see the problem of violent extremism remaining in the region . . . beyond even this current threat of [ISIS]."[10]

the Joint Staff. He also commented on what he foresaw for ISIS in the future. "What I expect [ISIS] to do is to look for other things to do—to pick up and move elsewhere. So I in no way want to suggest that we have effectively contained . . . the threat posed by [ISIS]."[11]

It would not be long before ISIS provided evidence of how accurate Mayville's predictions were. On August 19, masked militants beheaded US journalist James Foley in the infamous videotaped execution that quickly went viral. People everywhere were reminded that ISIS was far from finished—and that it was ready to respond to any international opposition.

CHAPTER SIX

CAMPAIGN
OF TERROR

When ISIS released footage of Foley's beheading, militants titled the video "A Message to America." Both Foley and his executioner delivered parts of this message to the camera. For his part, the journalist noted that, when US forces began conducting air strikes against ISIS, "They signed my death certificate."[1]

The ISIS extremist who killed Foley—Jihadi John—echoed similar ideas. In addition, Jihadi John indicated the life of another US journalist, Steven Sotloff, hung in the balance. "The life of this American citizen, Obama, depends on your next decision," warned the masked ISIS militant.[2] Based on his message,

Several experts who reviewed the tape of Foley's beheading indicated that Foley, *right*, was probably forced to recite much of what he said.

the president faced a choice: discontinue air strikes or deal with a direct threat to US citizens.

Prior to this point, part of ISIS's identity was wrapped up in its war against a near enemy. Unlike al-Qaeda, the terrorist organization was not specifically focused on targeting the United States or Europe. With Foley's taped execution, however, matters changed. Just as international leaders had declared their unwillingness to tolerate ISIS, ISIS had expressed its refusal to permit foreign interference.

ADDITIONAL EXECUTIONS

In the weeks ahead, the United States did not back down in its military opposition to ISIS. In response, militants once again relied upon social media to respond to US air strikes. On September 2, 2014, ISIS released another taped execution. This time, a man who sounded and appeared much like Jihadi John killed Sotloff as the camera rolled.

It would not be the last instance of ISIS launching an online campaign to dispatch a graphic warning to the world. Nor did the group limit its victims to US citizens. Citizens of any nation that supported Operation Inherent

نك سُتعيد جنودنا من العراق وأفغانستان إلى بيوتهم وأنك ستغلق سجن غوا

More videotaped beheadings meant other countries wanted to stop ISIS from spreading further.

Resolve appeared to be at risk. This was made obvious on September 13, when ISIS publicized its taped execution of British aid worker David Haines.

In the same video, a militant believed to be Jihadi John also threatened the United Kingdom with further violence. He stated that a second British hostage, Alan Henning, was at serious risk of sharing Haines's fate. He added that ISIS would kill Henning if British Prime Minister David Cameron continued his "evil alliance with America."[3] Similar to much of the international community, Cameron expressed sadness and horror at ISIS's murder of Haines. Still, he also reinforced the British people's resolve that the United Kingdom would not yield to a terrorist organization. "We have to confront this menace," Cameron said. "Step by step, we must drive back, dismantle, and ultimately destroy [ISIS] and what it stands for. . . . We will do so in a calm, deliberate way but with an iron determination."[4] By the end of September, opposition forces had continued bombing ISIS strongholds and had extended air strikes throughout Syria. Militants reacted

Cameron spoke out against ISIS's actions during the fall of 2014.

by releasing a video on October 3 that showed Henning being executed.

In the months that followed, ISIS kept up its persecution of various local groups throughout Syria and Iraq. Then, on November 13, the organization published a 17-minute audio message to its followers on its social media accounts. According to ISIS, the speaker in this recording was al-Baghdadi. During the speech, al-Baghdadi denounced the countries participating in Operation Inherent Resolve as "terrified, weak, and powerless." He also encouraged jihadists to take a more global approach to confronting their enemies. In emphasizing that point, al-Baghdadi told them to "light the Earth with fire upon all tyrants."[5]

Much as ISIS's videotaped executions had done, al-Baghdadi's audio recording served as ammunition for the group's social media campaign. Compared to older terrorist organizations, ISIS made far greater use of social media websites such as Facebook, Twitter, and YouTube. As a result, militants were better able to share information rapidly—and with a vaster audience. In addition, the shock value of the graphic content of ISIS's videos enhanced the speed with which they went viral.

On the one hand, jihadists had provoked international resistance from countries participating in Operation Inherent Resolve. On the other, they had figured out how to use social media as a microphone. In the face of ongoing air strikes and increasing foreign opposition, this microphone became one of ISIS's most valuable weapons.

MILITANTS' MESSAGES AND DEMANDS

As of early 2015, ISIS was no longer merely using hostage videos to retaliate against bombings and international interference. Terrorists had also

DIFFICULT DECISIONS ABOUT ISIS'S POSTS

Companies such as YouTube, Twitter, and Facebook were caught in the midst of a difficult situation when ISIS began posting videotaped executions. Allowing ISIS militants to publicize such activities was not an option. Doing so would inevitably make social media outlets channels for ISIS to spread its propaganda. On the other hand, censoring content raised questions about the social media sites' commitment to free speech.

For most social media companies, it was important to tread carefully between these two issues. In the case of YouTube, representatives explained they sometimes permitted questionable content to be posted. They said they mainly did this in situations when a video demonstrated "documentary or news value."

Nevertheless, YouTube removed the complete video of Sotloff's beheading within hours of it being posted. Spokespeople for the company later cited community guidelines they already had in place. These included rules against content that "incites violence, crime or hatred, depicts gratuitous violence."[6] YouTube also noted it attempts to deactivate any accounts held by people with links to known terrorist organizations.

started relying upon social media to make more specific demands. Proof of this occurred on January 20, when ISIS militants published new video footage. In a taped recording, they demanded $200 million from the Japanese government within 72 hours.[7] If officials refused to pay, a masked jihadist believed to be Jihadi John threatened to harm two Japanese hostages.

Japan's prime minister, Shinzo Abe, had recently pledged $200 million to aid refugees displaced by ISIS. Abe explained this donation would ideally help restore "peace and stability" in Iraq and Syria.[8] Unlike nations such as the United States and the United Kingdom, Japan had not taken an active role in air strikes against ISIS. Yet Abe and other Japanese officials nonetheless voiced their support of efforts to overpower the militants.

Inevitably, Japan refused to bow to ISIS's demands. In turn, jihadists published another gruesome video on social media sites on January 24. During this footage, they displayed the severed head of kidnapped private military contractor Haruna Yukawa.

ISIS militants also insisted on revised terms surrounding the potential surrender of a different

Japanese hostage, journalist Kenji Goto. Specifically, they ordered that the Jordanian government first free one of its political prisoners, Sajida al-Rishawi. Roughly one decade earlier, al-Rishawi had been involved in terrorist attacks that took place in Jordan. Authorities determined she and her husband were working for al-Qaeda when they attempted to carry out a series of hotel bombings. They claimed al-Rishawi was the sister of a close comrade of al-Zarqawi, who had formed AQI.

If al-Rishawi was freed, ISIS discussed the possibility they would release a second hostage—Jordanian military pilot Moath al-Kasasbeh. It is likely militants captured al-Kasasbeh when his plane crashed in Syria in December 2014. Yet after hearing ISIS's proposal, Jordanian officials were not convinced. They wanted proof al-Kasasbeh was still alive, which they believed ISIS failed to offer. Instead, on February 3, ISIS responded to Jordan's hesitation with

70

Air strikes in Syria were launched in hopes of destroying ISIS's weapons and training sites.

different and far more disturbing evidence. On that date, ISIS published a video and still images of the pilot being burned to death in a cage. Just days before, the group had also released footage of Goto's headless body.

The Jordanian government did not take long to react to al-Kasasbeh's murder. By February 5, it retaliated by launching air strikes over Raqqa, Syria. Jordanian military forces targeted locations ISIS

"I DIRECT A MESSAGE TO OUR GENEROUS BROTHERS OF [ISIS] IN SYRIA: TO HOST MY SON . . . WITH GENEROUS HOSPITALITY. I ASK GOD THAT THEIR HEARTS ARE GATHERED TOGETHER WITH LOVE, AND THAT HE IS RETURNED TO HIS FAMILY, WIFE, AND MOTHER. WE ARE ALL MUSLIMS."[10]

—SAFI YOUSEF AL-KASASBEH, FATHER OF ISIS HOSTAGE MOATH AL-KASASBEH

COMPLEX OPPOSITION TO A CAMPAIGN OF TERROR

As ISIS continued its campaign of terror throughout 2015, foreign nations—including the United States—were often forced to carefully consider their responses. In many cases, their reactions were shaped by other conflicts that were also brewing in the Middle East. In Iraq, for example, Kurdistan was already self-governing, but many Kurds wanted complete independence from the Iraqi government. Yet it was possible their efforts would lead to even greater political instability in the region. In turn, this made it more difficult for the United States to directly aid Kurdish forces fighting ISIS. On the one hand, it was important for the Kurds to be able to battle extremists. On the other, strengthening Kurdish troops would also potentially bolster their ability to divide Iraq.

Iran presented a further complexity for US officials trying to oppose ISIS. Iranian Shiites were eager to overpower the terrorist organization. At the same time, however, Iran's Shiite warriors had long been at odds with US forces. They had also been accused of various human rights abuses. As a result, the United States was compelled to tread cautiously between striking at ISIS and assisting Iran.

used to store ammunition and train militants. Soon, other nations would join Jordan in intensifying their efforts to defeat the jihadists. Meanwhile, ISIS continued spreading its message of Islamic extremism, promoting terrorism, and recruiting followers from every corner of the globe.

MORE TO THE STORY

THE AFTERMATH OF MOATH AL-KASASBEH'S DEATH

The Jordanian government by no means reacted passively to the execution of al-Kasasbeh. Shortly after ISIS released video and still images of the pilot's death, Jordanian officials ordered two of AQI's own prisoners killed. One was al-Rishawi—the AQI operative whom ISIS militants had hoped to see released. Jordanians also executed Ziad Karbouli, who had once served as a top aide to AQI leader al-Zarqawi. Meanwhile, angry crowds took to Jordan's streets, crying out for revenge for the murder of al-Kasasbeh.

"Those who doubted the atrocities committed by ISIS now have the proof," remarked Jordanian government spokesperson Mohammad al-Momani. "Those who doubted Jordan's power will soon see the proof, as well. [Al-Kasasbeh's] blood will not be shed in vain."

On February 5, 2015, Jordanian forces also responded to al-Kasasbeh's execution with air strikes against ISIS targets in Syria. Yet some experts predicted that, moving forward, militants would suffer worse consequences. "The propaganda factor, I think, is going to completely backfire on them," observed a US law enforcement analyst. "When was the last time you had a mob in the street of one of these Muslim countries that was not screaming 'death to America,' but [that was] in fact screaming, 'get revenge on ISIS'? . . . I think it's a huge mistake on the part of ISIS."[1]

CHAPTER SEVEN

WINNING
WORLDWIDE
SUPPORT

E arly on, the bulk of extremists who joined
ISIS were from Iraq and Syria. As time passed,
however, that changed. In some cases, ISIS forced
membership upon people via techniques such as
kidnapping, threats, and brainwashing. It also relied
upon social media outlets to win international followers.

In early 2015, US officials reported approximately
4,000 foreign recruits had joined ISIS's ranks. Those
numbers did not include the estimated thousands
of Iraqis and Syrians who supported the terrorist
organization.[1] Despite air strikes led by certain nations

As ISIS gained territory and power, Westerners and children joined the
extremists in their cause.

from Operation Inherent Resolve, ISIS had failed to crumble as of June 2015. Some military and political experts speculated a lack of ground troops was allowing militants to recover from foreign attacks. Yet several people perceived that an even larger problem was the steady stream of new members. Further complicating matters was the challenge of determining how many jihadists air strikes were actually eliminating.

"When it comes time to killing people, the only way to really confirm it, you need boots on the ground or eyeballs on the target," said Christopher Harmer, an analyst with the Institute for the Study of War in Washington, DC. "As long as ISIS shows the ability to continue to recruit foreign fighters and regenerate lost manpower, then it's an irrelevant metric. I don't know how

CUBS OF ISIS

According to the UN, recruiting child fighters is regarded as a war crime. Yet it did not take long for ISIS to begin building an army of extremely young warriors. In some cases, these jihadists were reported to be no more than six or seven years old. ISIS started training these "cubs of the Islamic State" in special camps throughout Iraq and Syria.[2]

In most situations, children either volunteer or are enrolled by their parents. While at ISIS's camps, they learn how to care for and fire machine guns. They also practice carrying out executions by beheading dolls. When they complete training, these young fighters sometimes work at checkpoints. They are also frequently used as human shields and as participants in suicide missions.

long ISIS can sustain battlefield damage . . . but so far they haven't collapsed."[3]

GAINING FOLLOWERS AND FORGING ALLIANCES

The issue of why international recruits were flocking to ISIS was also complex. What was clearer was that men and women from many different places were joining the group. From British schoolgirls to US and Canadian medical students, such individuals often left behind perplexed family and friends. They frequently traveled through border crossings in Turkey, burned their passports, and eagerly began a new life with ISIS.

Both terrorism experts and psychologists alike suggested multiple reasons for the organization's powerful

BECOMING A BRIDE OF ISIS

By late 2014, roughly 300 young women from Europe and the United States had attempted to join ISIS. According to terrorism experts, militants recruited many of these individuals with the same promises they used to enlist other followers. They spoke of a rewarding life in the caliphate and the glory of martyrdom. ISIS recruiters also attracted the women—several of whom were teenagers—by describing how they would be wives to heroic warriors. Via online video messages, the terrorist organization encouraged prospective "brides of ISIS" to prepare for the future.[4] Recruiters instructed them to learn how to cook, sew, and provide first aid treatment. Often running away from home, female jihadists heeded their call and boarded planes bound for the Middle East.

influence on young people around the world. In many instances, ISIS lured in followers with promises of wealth and status within the new caliphate. Recruiters also seemed to play upon members' desire to be part of a meaningful and glorious adventure. To this end, they created propaganda videos that documented their successes on the battlefield. Finally, ISIS assured prospective jihadists that, even if they perished fighting for the caliphate, their reward in the afterlife would be great. The group essentially spread a message that offered acceptance and prosperity.

"Before I [came] . . . to Syria . . . it wasn't like I was some anarchist . . . who just wants to destroy the world and kill everybody," remarked former Canadian citizen Andre Poulin. "I was a regular person." In 2013, Poulin left home for the Middle East to join ISIS. He later participated in propaganda videos that helped recruit additional members. "We need . . . engineers, we need doctors, [and] we need professionals," Poulin proclaimed. "Every person can contribute something to [ISIS]."[5]

Thanks to ISIS's mastery of social media, this message reached potential followers on an extremely wide scale.

In March 2015, the US State Department estimated the organization was using its Twitter accounts to share 90,000 tweets a day. Officials admitted that ISIS's online recruitment abilities were "something we have not seen before."[6]

To counter militants' increased foreign membership, national governments set a variety of counterplans into action. In several European countries, for example, lawmakers created legislation that made support of ISIS a punishable offense. And in the United States, anti-ISIS messaging campaigns were established to talk young people out of joining the jihadists.

Nevertheless, ISIS continued to flourish. In February 2015, the DOD announced that ISIS consisted of as many as 30,000 fighters.[7] It was increasing the strength of terrorist cells in politically unstable nations such as Yemen. Along the way, ISIS was also winning the loyalty of separate terrorist groups such as Boko Haram.

"WE ARE WAY BEHIND. [ISIS IS] FAR SUPERIOR AND [MORE] ADVANCED THAN WE ARE WHEN IT COMES TO NEW MEDIA TECHNOLOGIES."[8]

—MAAJID NAWAZ, FORMER JIHADIST AND AUTHOR OF *RADICAL: MY JOURNEY OUT OF ISLAMIST EXTREMISM*

FROM THE
HEADLINES

FOREIGN FIGHTERS
LOYAL TO ISIS

Since its creation, ISIS has managed to maintain a large following in a wide variety of Asian, African, and Western nations. By early 2015, the fact that so many foreign fighters had left their homes to become ISIS militants shocked many people. It also made international news headlines.

Based on recent research, by the spring of 2015, roughly 20,000 additional fighters from nearly 80 nations had joined extremists in the Middle East. It is likely many of these men and women lent their support to ISIS. According to the British Broadcasting Corporation, approximately one-fourth of foreign extremists in Iraq and Syria were from Western countries. The rest were believed to have relocated there from nearby Arab nations. Terrorism experts have listed Tunisia, Saudi Arabia, Russia, Jordan, and Morocco as the top five sources of foreign extremists in Iraq and Syria. Yet ISIS has also won followers from several other areas, including France, Germany, the United Kingdom, the United States, and Canada.[9]

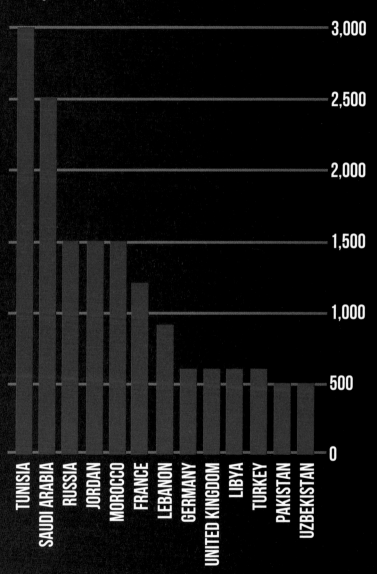

FOREIGN FIGHTERS IN SYRIA AND IRAQ

Any country featuring fewer than 500 individuals who left home to join extremists in Syria and Iraq was omitted from the chart.

NUMBER OF FIGHTERS

3,000
2,500
2,000
1,500
1,000
500
0

TUNISIA
SAUDI ARABIA
RUSSIA
JORDAN
MOROCCO
FRANCE
LEBANON
GERMANY
UNITED KINGDOM
LIBYA
TURKEY
PAKISTAN
UZBEKISTAN

During the 1990s, Islamic extremists in Nigeria formed Boko Haram. On March 7, 2015, Boko Haram's leader—Abubakar Shekau—swore allegiance to ISIS in an audiotaped message. Less than one week later, ISIS released an audio statement of its own. In this recording, militants welcomed Boko Haram's backing and declared the caliphate had grown to encompass western Africa.

For ISIS, such a partnership further extended its international reach. For Boko Haram, the alliance was a promise of enhanced support, funding, and recruitment abilities. A link to ISIS earned smaller terrorist groups increased respect from jihadists. It also made them more widely recognized—and feared—throughout the international community.

HOW BOKO HARAM OPERATES

According to members of Boko Haram, it is *haram*, or "forbidden," for Muslims to participate in any activities connected to Western society.[10] Similar to ISIS, this Nigerian terrorist organization formed with ambitions of overthrowing the government and building a caliphate. It also relied on a wide range of terrorist activities to achieve its goals. Boko Haram earned a reputation for carrying out bombings, armed invasions, and kidnappings. In April 2014, the group made international headlines when militants abducted approximately 300 schoolgirls from Chibok, Nigeria.[11] Several of these young women remain missing today. It is believed many were forced to convert to Islam and marry Boko Haram fighters.

The abduction of hundreds of girls by Boko Haram brought awareness to the horrific practices of the Nigerian extremist group.

SEVERAL SOURCES OF FUNDING

In addition to having robust membership, ISIS had also demonstrated it was able to obtain steady funding. Winning new territory and recruits amidst air strikes was a costly effort. Yet, since its creation, ISIS had managed to maintain its weapons and supplies.

According to Kurdish officials, the group was earning as much as $6 million on a daily basis.[12] Some of this money came from oil fields ISIS seized throughout Iraq and Syria. Militants also depended upon taxes they imposed on the millions of people living in the areas they controlled by early 2015. ISIS fighters quickly earned a reputation for robbing banks, stealing livestock, and even snatching jewelry off women's necks. Extortion and ransom were examples of additional methods ISIS used to generate income. When possible, the organization made deals in cash, which posed challenges for outside parties attempting to track its financial activities.

ISIS also received support from wealthy private donors all over the world. Many countries, including the United States, criminalized providing financial aid to terrorist organizations. Nevertheless, not every nation strictly enforced this policy. As of late 2014, US analysts considered Kuwait and Qatar "trouble spots when it [came] to counterterrorist financing enforcement."[13]

Another major source of ISIS's funding was the thousands of archaeological sites under its control in the Middle East. Private collectors and dealers proved willing to pay top prices

"THE FIRST PHONE CALL YOU MAKE ONCE YOU CROSS THE BORDERS IS ONE OF THE MOST DIFFICULT THINGS YOU WILL EVER HAVE TO DO. YOUR PARENTS ARE ALREADY WORRIED ENOUGH OVER WHERE YOU ARE. . . . HOWEVER, WHEN YOU HEAR THEM SOB AND BEG LIKE CRAZY . . . FOR YOU TO COME BACK, IT'S SO HARD. . . . BUT AS LONG AS YOU ARE FIRM, AND YOU KNOW THIS IS ALL FOR THE SAKE OF ALLAH, THEN NOTHING CAN SHAKE YOU."[14]

—ISIS RECRUITER (FORMERLY FROM SCOTLAND)

for artifacts that sometimes dated back to 9,000 BCE. Archaeologists estimated hundreds of millions of dollars were changing hands for stolen tablets and manuscripts. "It is the looting of the very roots of humanity, artifacts from the oldest civilizations in the world," observed Iraqi archaeologist Abdulamir al-Hamdani. "A shrine, a tomb, a church, a palace or an archaeological site is dug up. They will sell the useful objects and destroy the rest."[15]

Most financial experts believed that such activities could not fund terrorists forever. Eventually, certain areas within ISIS's caliphate gave signs of experiencing an economic downturn. At the same time, however, the organization's budget did not appear likely to collapse in the immediate future. As a result, the question of how long ISIS could endure remained difficult to predict by the summer of 2015.

CHAPTER EIGHT

EVALUATING
ISIS'S FUTURE

A s of June 2015, the international crisis involving ISIS seemed at a standstill. ISIS was still holding strong in terms of funding and recruits. Yet participants in Operation Inherent Resolve showed little indication of backing down. In February 2015, President Obama formally requested that Congress authorize his use of military force against ISIS. In his petition to lawmakers, Obama insisted he still had no intention of deploying ground troops. Nevertheless, he wanted Congress to grant him the power to order "ground combat operations in limited circumstances."[1] Per the president, these included rescue missions and action taken to target ISIS leadership. In his letter to legislators,

ISIS continued to have a stronghold in the Middle East in 2015.

Obama also suggested limiting ongoing military action against the jihadists to a period of three years.

Lawmakers' initial reactions to President Obama's petition varied greatly. Some thought it was too broad in the terms it set. Others believed it was important not to limit Obama's authority to deal with ISIS. Meanwhile, as a legislative debate raged on in Washington, DC, militants continued an unpredictable campaign throughout the Middle East.

"HISTORY HAS SHOWN THE DANGERS THAT MILLIONS CAN BE PLACED IN IF OUR LEADERS DON'T FACE DOWN A LOOMING THREAT BY CALLING IT WHAT IT IS AND PUTTING OUR FULL WEIGHT BEHIND EFFORTS TO VANQUISH IT. . . . UNLESS WE ALL WANT THINGS TO GET A WHOLE LOT WORSE BEFORE THEY MIGHT GET ANY BETTER, THE UNITED STATES WILL HAVE TO DEPLOY CONSIDERABLY MORE . . . 'KINETIC' RESOURCES [MILITARY INITIATIVES] TO PUT [VICTORY] IN SIGHT."[2]

—RETIRED US GENERALS MICHAEL FLYNN AND JAMES LIVINGSTON AND CONGRESSIONAL COUNTERTERRORISM ADVISER MICHAEL SMITH

TWISTS AND TURNS WITHIN THE CALIPHATE

In the spring of 2015, ISIS appeared to offer a few unexpected signs of hope as far as its prisoners were concerned. On March 1, militants released 19 Christians they had kidnapped from northern Syria

Most of the Yazidi prisoners released were extremely old, young, or ill.

the week before. Then, on April 8, jihadists freed more than 200 Yazidi captives.[3]

Spokespeople for ISIS did not cite the organization's reasons for these surprising displays of mercy. Some terrorism experts pointed to the likelihood that the releases were the result of negotiations between militants and Sunni tribal leaders. They suggested ISIS was attempting to build better relations with the Sunnis.

Yet another possibility was that the prisoners had been freed due to the decrees of sharia judges. As militants developed a caliphate throughout Iraq and Syria, they established a court system based on sharia law. Certain terrorism experts believed judges had ordered various

AIR STRIKES AND UNINTENTIONAL CASUALTIES

In 2014, the United States and other members of Operation Inherent Resolve began conducting air strikes to destroy ISIS. Yet some sources subsequently accused them of hitting civilians as well. In April 2015, the Syrian Observatory for Human Rights (SOHR) commented on the toll the bombings have taken since September 2014. According to SOHR, air strikes had killed at least 2,000 people in Syria. They estimated that, of those 2,000, roughly 66 of the casualties were civilians.[4]

Even before these numbers were released, the US Central Command (CENTCOM) admitted to investigating reports of civilian deaths. In February 2015, CENTCOM spokesperson Major Curtis Kellogg acknowledged rumors of unintentional casualties caused by the air strikes. "We take all allegations of civilian casualties seriously," remarked Kellogg. "And we apply very rigorous standards in our targeting process to avoid . . . civilian casualties in the first place. Our efforts stand in stark contrast to the tactics of [ISIS] . . . who [continue] to kill, torture, and abuse civilians, as well as embed their combatants in civilian areas."[5]

hostages be released because they did not pose any military opposition to ISIS.

Regardless of these liberations, ISIS by no means ceased its terrorist activities. ISIS militants were advancing into other politically unstable areas, including Libya and Yemen. Along the way, they carried out additional bombings and public executions to demonstrate their authority.

Meanwhile, supporters of ISIS living in far-off areas hatched terror plots across the globe. In March 2015, authorities arrested an Illinois national guardsman, Hasan Edmonds, and his cousin, Jonas Edmonds, for planning an attack in ISIS's name. The pair had allegedly

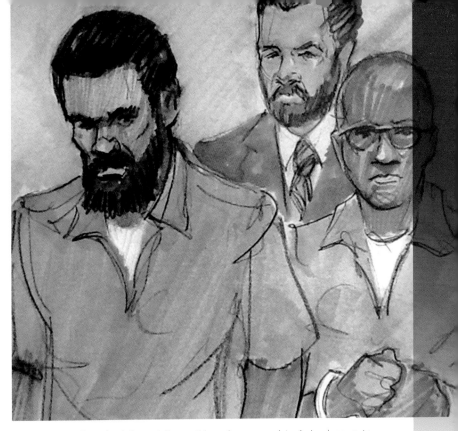

Jonas Edmonds, *left*, and Hasan Edmonds appeared in federal court in Chicago for conspiring with ISIS.

been organizing an armed assault on a military facility in the northern part of the state. Both men—who were US citizens—had also been eager to join ISIS fighters in the Middle East.

In this case, thanks to increased government surveillance, tragedy had been prevented. Opponents of ISIS hoped closely monitoring its international followers via their social media activities would help further weaken the group. At the same time, US forces and their allies kept using air strikes to pound targets in Iraq and Syria.

In addition to these efforts, local ground troops remained engaged in combat with ISIS militants.

Then, in late April 2015, reporters with the British newspaper the *Guardian* made an announcement regarding al-Baghdadi. Based on what they had learned from both a Western and an Iraqi source, the caliph had been seriously wounded. Details regarding the story were still vague. Yet the journalists indicated al-Baghdadi had been hit during a US air strike the previous month. Supposedly, he had suffered a significant spinal injury when the car he had been traveling in was hit in Baghdad. Though al-Baghdadi had survived, he was reported to be unable to move.

For enemies of ISIS, this news, if accurate, marked an achievement in their battle against the jihadists. Nevertheless, few people believed it symbolized an end to the terrorist organization. As al-Baghdadi recovered, a temporary leader, Abu Alaa al-Afri, assumed control of ISIS. Based on what some sources indicated, al-Afri was a "rising star" who would become caliph in the event that al-Baghdadi died.[6]

Smoke rises after a US air strike targets ISIS militants outside Mosul, Iraq, in August 2014.

FROM THE HEADLINES

TAKING CREDIT FOR TERRORISM IN FRANCE

In early January 2015, a series of terrorist attacks rocked Paris, France. First, on January 7, Hamyd Mourad and brothers Said and Cherif Kouachi stormed the office of the French satirical publication *Charlie Hebdo*. Once inside, they shot 11 staff members and, as they escaped, killed a police officer. The men carried out the executions in response to cartoons published by *Charlie Hebdo* they considered disrespectful to the prophet Muhammad. Mourad ultimately turned himself in, and the Kouachis died in a standoff with police the following Friday.

On Thursday, January 8, suspects Amedy Coulibaly and Hayat Boumeddiene shot a police officer in a Paris suburb. The following day, they took 19 people hostage in a Jewish supermarket. Four hostages were killed, Coulibaly died amidst police gunfire, and Boumeddiene managed to get away.[7]

In the aftermath of the attacks, both al-Qaeda in the Arabian Peninsula (AQAP) and ISIS boasted of helping orchestrate the violence. While it is still not clear which one deserves more credit, ISIS wasted no time in releasing messages that glorified the bloodshed. In addition, the group urged its followers to continue waging jihad throughout Europe and the United States.

The attacks at the *Charlie Hebdo* office were a shock to people around the world.

> "I WAS SHOCKED BY WHAT I DID. . . . IT'S NOT ISLAM. DON'T GIVE YOUR LIFE UP FOR NOTHING."[9]
>
> —FORMER ISIS MILITANT

A LOOK AT LONG-TERM SOLUTIONS

At present, far more remains unclear about the future of ISIS than who will head the organization. President Obama said in early 2015 that the militants were "on the defensive" and were "going to lose."[8] But ISIS still maintains control of far more territory than it has lost to opposition forces.

Since the organization's creation, ISIS has shocked the world with attempted genocides and videotaped beheadings. It has spread a message of Islamic extremism with incredible and unanticipated speed. In the process, ISIS has both made international enemies and won worldwide recruits.

There are no guarantees if or when ISIS will fall from power. Nor is there any way to accurately predict how many lives will be changed or lost in the meantime. What is certain is that military action alone will not be enough to overcome ISIS. Equally important is evaluating what situations allowed it to develop and thrive.

Political instability and the security vacuum it supports are both contributing factors. So is underestimating how rapidly radical ideas and activities can gain popularity on a global scale. Misunderstanding and discrimination between different religious and ethnic groups have further fueled ISIS's growth.

In the long term, more than air strikes and combat missions will be needed to defeat militants. Ultimately, open dialogue between people of many different backgrounds will be necessary as well. Becoming more informed about ISIS—from what it stands for to the threat it poses—is also an important

INCREASING EFFORTS TO OVERCOME ISIS

In late April 2015, members of Operation Inherent Resolve began discussing the likelihood of having to broaden their campaign. With ISIS expanding into other nations, some officials expressed concerns that current strategies would not be enough to overcome the terrorist group. Part of their worries stemmed from the growing number of smaller terrorist organizations that have pledged allegiance to ISIS.

Boko Haram is one example of such a group. Militants in Libya, Egypt, Afghanistan, and the Philippines have also attempted to form ties with ISIS. In many cases, such terrorist cells have received funding and military support in exchange for their loyalty. In turn, several have declared the areas they operate out of to be "provinces" of ISIS.

If this pattern continues, members of Operation Inherent Resolve will be forced to extend protection, surveillance, and outreach on a wider scale. As they decide how to address ISIS's future progress, most believe they will need to keep attacking militants on multiple levels. This will likely involve a combination of enhanced air strikes and efforts to cripple the terrorists' funding and recruitment abilities.

step. As such, a combination of action, communication, and knowledge are critical to addressing ISIS both now and in the future.

THE IDENTITY OF ISIS'S NEXT CALIPH

Described as a compelling person, the man who might potentially be al-Baghdadi's successor is a former physics teacher. Similar to many of the details surrounding al-Baghdadi's life, much about Abu Alaa al-Afri remains a mystery. Yet Iraqi government adviser Hisham al-Hishimi declared him to be "more important . . . smarter, and with better relationships" than al-Baghdadi.[10]

Nevertheless, as of April 2015, some sources questioned whether the current caliph was as badly injured as was originally reported. Others pointed out that ISIS relies upon an extremely elaborate process to determine the leader of the caliphate. A special council typically appoints the caliph, not the current man holding the title. "The position of caliph requires the right family and tribal connections to the prophet Muhammad and credentials as an Islamist scholar," noted Central Intelligence Agency (CIA) Middle East expert Bruce Riedel. "That's much more complicated than [simply] finding another terrorist."[11]

ISIS continues to grow each day, but as more countries work together, these allies have hope they can stop ISIS from establishing a caliphate.

ESSENTIAL
FACTS

MAJOR EVENTS

- In April 2013, the Islamic State in Iraq and Syria (ISIS) officially forms after years of evolving as an offshoot of al-Qaeda. Militants unite their Islamic extremism and their pursuit of jihad to defend their faith and expand their kingdom.

- Between the spring of 2013 and the summer of 2014, ISIS overtakes numerous villages, cities, and oil fields throughout Iraq and Syria.

- In August 2014, US president Barack Obama orders a series of air strikes against ISIS targets in Iraq.

- As of early 2015, experts estimate ISIS has a fighting force of up to 30,000 individuals.

KEY PLAYERS

- ISIS militants led by al-Baghdadi and who include jihadists from all over the world.

- Groups such as the Yazidis, Christians, Shiites, and Turkmen who are persecuted by ISIS.

- Foreign hostages who are taken by ISIS soldiers.

- The members of Operation Inherent Resolve who seek to defeat ISIS via military action and efforts to cripple the group's funding and recruitment abilities.

IMPACT ON SOCIETY

ISIS and other terrorist organizations formed allegiances that helped expand the caliphate. Vast numbers of Iraqis and Syrians became the victims of widespread displacement and violence. International leaders were forced to evaluate if and how they would respond to the terrorist threat ISIS poses. Everyday people from all walks of life—and every corner of the globe—have become increasingly concerned about the threat of terrorism within their communities.

QUOTE

"You are no longer fighting an insurgency. We are an Islamic army, and a State that has been accepted by a large number of Muslims worldwide. . . . So any attempt by you, Obama, to deny the Muslims their rights . . . will result in the bloodshed of your people."

—Jihadi John [Mohammed Emwazi]

GLOSSARY

AIR STRIKE
An attack such as a bombing that is made via aircraft.

COALITION
An alliance created for the purpose of organizing combined action.

DIPLOMATIC
Related to a job or activity that involves managing international relations.

EXTORTION
The act of obtaining something (especially money) through force or threats.

EXTREMIST
Related to extreme or fanatical political or religious views.

GENOCIDE
The deliberate killing of a large group of people, especially those of a particular ethnic or religious group.

HUMANITARIAN

Concerned with or seeking to promote human welfare.

IDEOLOGY

A system of ideas and ideals, especially one that forms the basis of political or economic policies.

INFIDEL

A person who does not believe in a particular organized religion.

INSURGENCY

A rebellion or violent attempt to take control of a government.

MARTYRDOM

The act of suffering or dying on account of one's religious beliefs.

PROPAGANDA

Information that persuades or pressures others.

RADICAL

In favor of complete political or social reform.

SANCTION

An order given to force a country to obey international laws.

ADDITIONAL
RESOURCES

SELECTED BIBLIOGRAPHY

Bostom, Andrew G., ed. *The Legacy of Jihad: Islamic Holy War and the Fate of Non-Muslims.* Amherst, NY: Prometheus, 2005. Print.

Sekulow, Jay. *The Rise of ISIS: The Coming Massacre.* New York: Howard, 2014. Print.

FURTHER READINGS

Cockburn, Patrick. *The Rise of Islamic State: ISIS and the New Sunni Revolution.* London: Verso, 2015. Print.

Gunter, Michael M. *The Kurds: A Modern History.* Princeton, NJ: Markus Weiner, 2015. Print.

Stern, Jessica. *ISIS: The State of Terror.* London: William Collins, 2015. Print.

WEBSITES

To learn more about Special Reports, visit **booklinks.abdopublishing.com**. These links are routinely monitored and updated to provide the most current information available.

FOR MORE INFORMATION

For more information on this subject, contact or visit the following organizations:

Refugees International
2001 S Street NW, Suite 700
Washington, DC 20009
800-733-8433
http://refugeesinternational.org/who-we-are
Refugees International advocates for aid and protection that benefits refugees from various war-torn nations. Since ISIS gained power in Iraq and Syria, it has worked to help displaced men, women, and children in those countries.

The United Nations (UN)
760 United Nations Plaza
New York, NY 10017
212-963-4475
http://www.un.org/en/index.html
The UN addresses various humanitarian issues on a global scale. It also takes steps to deal with terrorist organizations, including ISIS, that threaten international human rights.

SOURCE
NOTES

CHAPTER 1. A MENACING MESSAGE

1. Guy Adams. "Five Minutes of Savagery and a Video as Slick as It Is Sickening: How Evil Footage Reveals the True Savagery of ISIS." *Daily Mail*. Associated Newspapers, 21 Aug. 2014. Web. 17 June 2015.

2. Paula Mejia. "Remembering James Foley." *Newsweek*. Newsweek, 20 Aug. 2014. Web. 17 June 2015.

3. "ISIS Fast Facts." *CNN*. Cable News Network, 9 June 2015. Web. 17 June 2015.

4. "Statement by the President." *Embassy of the United States*. US Department of States, 20 Aug. 2014. Web. 17 June 2015.

CHAPTER 2. ORIGINS OF A TERRORIST ORGANIZATION

1. "Background: Al Qaeda." *Frontline*. WGBH Educational Foundation, 2015. Web. 17 June 2015.

2. "September 11th Fast Facts." *CNN*. Cable News Network, 27 Mar. 2015. Web. 17 June 2015.

3. Steve Schifferes. "US Says 'Coalition of Willing' Grows." *BBC News*. BBC, 21 Mar. 2003. Web. 17 June 2015.

4. "Saddam Hussein." *Bio*. A&E Television Networks, 2015. Web. 17 June 2015.

5. "Iraq Profile—Timeline." *BBC News*. BBC, 18 May 2015. Web. 17 June 2015.

6. "Sunnis and Shia in the Middle East." *BBC News*. BBC, 19 Dec. 2013. Web. 17 June 2015.

7. Kenneth Katzman. "Iraq: Politics, Security, and US Policy." *Congressional Research Service*. Congressional Research Service, 26 May 2015. Web. 17 June 2015.

8. Jason Keyser. "Camp Bucca: Military Closes Largest Detention Camp in Iraq." *World Post*. HuffingtonPost.com, 25 May 2011. Web. 17 June 2015.

9. Terrence McCoy. "How the Islamic State Evolved in an American Prison." *Washington Post*. Washington Post, 4 Nov. 2014. Web. 17 June 2015.

10. Rania el Gamal. "Analysis: Iraq Resumes Political Strife in Vacuum Left by US." *Reuters*. Thomson Reuters, 18 Dec. 2011. Web. 17 June 2015.

CHAPTER 3. NEW AND UNDENIABLY DANGEROUS

1. "Syria: The Story of the Conflict." *BBC News*. BBC, 12 Mar. 2015. Web. 17 June 2015.

2. F. Michael Maloof. "Now ISIS Expected to Snub al-Qaida." *WND Faith*. WND.com, 24 Nov. 2014. Web. 17 June 2015.

3. "Jabhat al-Nusra." *Mapping Militant Organizations*. Stanford University, 2015. Web. 17 June 2015.

4. Arwa Damon and Holly Yan. "Inside the Mind of an ISIS Fighter." *CNN*. Cable News Network, 4 Sept. 2014. Web. 17 June 2015.

5. Krishnadev Calamur. "ISIS: An Islamist Group Too Extreme Even for al-Qaida." *NPR*. NPR, 13 Jun. 2014. Web. 17 June 2015.

6. Laura Smith-Spark and Nic Robertson. "The Siege of Mosul: What's Happening? Why Is It Significant?" *CNN*. Cable News Network, 13 Jun. 2014. Web. 17 June 2015.

7. Nina Porzucki. "Ever Wonder What the Black-and-White ISIS Flag Means?" *PRI*. Public Radio International, 15 Dec. 2014. Web. 17 June 2015.

8. Jim Sciutto, Nic Robertson, and Laura Smith-Spark. "Recording: ISIS Promises More Fighting in More Iraqi Cities." *CNN*. Cable News Network, 12 June 2014. Web. 17 June 2015.

9. "Iraq Crisis: Militants 'Seize Tikrit' after Taking Mosul." *BBC News*. BBC, 11 June 2014. Web. 17 June 2015.

10. Ibid.

11. Arwa Damon and Holly Yan. "Inside the Mind of an ISIS Fighter." *CNN*. Cable News Network, 4 Sept. 2014. Web. 17 June 2015.

CHAPTER 4. LASTING IMPACTS

1. "Iraq Crisis: Militants 'Seize Tikrit' after Taking Mosul." *BBC News*. BBC, 11 June 2014. Web. 17 June 2015.

2. "Who Are the Kurds?" *BBC News*. BBC, 21 Oct. 2014. Web. 17 June 2015.

3. Salma Abdelaziz. "Syrian Radicals 'Brainwash' Kidnapped Kurdish Schoolchildren." *CNN*. Cable News Network, 26 June 2014. Web. 17 June 2015.

4. Joshua Berlinger. "Who Are the Religious and Ethnic Groups under Threat from ISIS?" *CNN*. Cable News Network, 8 Aug. 2014. Web. 17 June 2015.

5. Salma Abdelaziz. "Syrian Radicals 'Brainwash' Kidnapped Kurdish Schoolchildren." *CNN*. Cable News Network, 26 June 2014. Web. 17 June 2015.

6. Joshua Berlinger. "Who Are the Religious and Ethnic Groups under Threat from ISIS?" *CNN*. Cable News Network, 8 Aug. 2014. Web. 17 June 2015.

7. Kirk Semple. "Yazidi Girls Seized by ISIS Speak out after Escape." *New York Times*. New York Times Company, 14 Nov. 2014. Web. 17 June 2015.

8. Ibid.

9. Richard Engel and James Novogrod. "ISIS Terror: Yazidi Woman Recalls Horrors of Slave Auction." *NBC News*. NBCNews.com, 13 Feb. 2015. Web. 17 June 2015.

10. "'We Had to Get Out': RT Talks to Iraqi Refugees from ISIS-Occupied Regions." *RT*. TV-Novosti, 13 Feb. 2014. Web. 17 June 2015.

11. Fazel Hawramy. "Winter Brings Fresh Threat to Iraq's Refugees Who Fled the ISIS Advance." *Guardian*. Guardian News, 6 Dec. 2014. Web. 17 June 2015.

12. Nick Thompson. "Iraq's Yazidis Trapped, Hiding from ISIS in the Mountains." *CNN*. Cable News Network, 8 Aug. 2014. Web. 17 June 2015.

13. Ibid.

CHAPTER 5. EARLY RESPONSES

1. "ISIS Fast Facts." *CNN*. Cable News Network, 9 June 2015. Web. 17 June 2015.

2. "Statement by the President." *White House*. White House, 7 Aug. 2014. Web. 17 June 2015.

3. Rebecca Kaplan. "Obama Says It Again: No Ground Troops in Iraq." *CBS News*. CBSNews.com, 17 Sept. 2014. Web. 17 June 2015.

4. Joel Landau. "British Prime Minister David Cameron on ISIS: 'We Have to Confront the Menace.'" *Daily News*. NYDailyNews.com, 14 Sept. 2014. Web. 17 June 2015.

5. Dana Ford and Josh Levs. "'Heroic' Mission Rescues Desperate Yazidis from ISIS." *CNN*. Cable News Network, 16 Aug. 2014. Web. 17 June 2015.

6. Barbara Starr. "US Officials Say 6,000 ISIS Fighters Killed in Battles." *CNN*. Cable News Network, 22 Jan. 2015. Web. 17 June 2015.

7. "Operation Inherent Resolve." *GlobalSecurity.org*. GlobalSecurity.org, 3 Sept. 2015. Web. 17 June 2015.

SOURCE NOTES
CONTINUED

8. "Security Council Adopts Resolution 2170 (2014) Condemning Gross, Widespread Abuse of Human Rights by Extremist Groups in Iraq, Syria." *United Nations.* United Nations, 15 Aug. 2014. Web. 17 June 2015.

9. Hunter Walker. "Obama: Military Mission in Iraq 'Will Be a Long-Term Project.'" *Business Insider.* Business Insider, 9 Aug. 2014. Web. 17 June 2015.

10. Carol Morello and Anne Gearan. "Around World, Mixed Reactions to US-Led Airstrikes in Syria." *Washington Post.* Washington Post, 23 Sept. 2014. Web. 17 June 2014.

11. Jon Harper. "General: Iraq Airstrikes Have Limited, 'Temporary Effect.'" *Stars and Stripes.* Stars and Stripes, 11 Aug. 2014. Web. 17 June 2015.

CHAPTER 6. CAMPAIGN OF TERROR
1. Rukmini Callimachi. "Militant Group Says It Killed American Journalist in Syria." *New York Times.* New York Times Company, 19 Aug. 2014. Web. 17 June 2015.

2. Ibid.

3. "ISIS Fast Facts." *CNN.* Cable News Network, 9 June 2015. Web. 17 June 2015.

4. Josh Levs and Jethro Mullen. "Britain Vows to 'Confront' the ISIS 'Menace' After Killing of David Haines." *CNN.* Cable News Network, 14 Sept. 2014. Web. 17 June 2015.

5. "ISIS Fast Facts." *CNN.* Cable News Network, 9 June 2015. Web. 17 June 2015.

6. Jeff Bercovici. "YouTube's Policies Are Clear: Beheading Is Not an Act of Free Speech." *Forbes.* Forbes, 3 Sept. 2014. Web. 17 June 2015.

7. Brian Todd, Joe Johns, and Jethro Mullen. "ISIS' Japanese Hostage Video Raises New Questions about 'Jihadi John.'" *CNN.* Cable News Network, 28 Jan. 2015. Web. 17 June 2015.

8. Ibid.

9. Martin Fackler. "Departing from Japan's Pacifism, Shinzo Abe Vows Revenge for Killings." *New York Times.* New York Times Company, 1 Feb. 2015. Web. 17 June 2015.

10. Omar Akour and Diaa Hadid. "Father of Pilot Captured by IS Pleads for Release." *USA Today.* Gannett Company, 25 Dec. 2014. Web. 17 June 2015.

11. Greg Botelho and Dana Ford. "Jordan Executes Prisoners after ISIS Hostage Burned Alive." *CNN.* Cable News Network, 4 Feb. 2015. Web. 17 June 2015.

CHAPTER 7. WINNING WORLDWIDE SUPPORT
1. Tim Mak and Nancy A. Youssef. "ISIS Ranks Grow as Fast as US Bombs Can Wipe Them Out." *Daily Beast.* Daily Beast Company, 3 Feb. 2015. Web. 17 June 2015.

2. Cassandra Vinograd, Ghazi Balkiz, and Ammar Cheikh Omar. "ISIS Trains Child Soldiers at Camps for 'Cubs of the Islamic State.'" *NBC News.* NBCNews.com, 7 Nov. 2014. Web. 17 June 2015.

3. Tim Mak and Nancy A. Youssef. "ISIS Ranks Grow as Fast as US Bombs Can Wipe Them Out." *Daily Beast*. Daily Beast Company, 3 Feb. 2015. Web. 17 June 2015.

4. Vivienne Walt. "Marriage and Martyrdom: How ISIS Is Winning Women." *TIME*. TIME, 18 Nov. 2014. Web. 17 June 2015.

5. Erin Banco. "Why Do People Join ISIS? The Psychology of a Terrorist." *International Business Times*. IBT Media, 5 Sept. 2014. Web. 17 June 2015.

6. Holly Yan. "How Is ISIS Luring Westerners?" *CNN*. Cable News Network, 23 Mar. 2015. Web. 17 June 2015.

7. "ISIS Fast Facts." *CNN*. Cable News Network, 9 June 2015. Web. 17 June 2015.

8. Holly Yan. "How Is ISIS Luring Westerners?" *CNN*. Cable News Network, 23 Mar. 2015. Web. 17 June 2015.

9. "Battle for Iraq and Syria in Maps." *BBC News*. BBC, 8 June 2015. Web. 17 June 2015.

10. Farouk Chothia. "Who Are Nigeria's Boko Haram Islamists?" *BBC News*. BBC, 4 May 2015. Web. 17 June 2015.

11. Jacqueline Klimas. "Boko Haram Kidnapped Nigeria Schoolgirls Likely Facing Forced Labor, Sexual Assault." *Washington Times*. Washington Times, 23 Dec. 2014. Web. 17 June 2015.

12. Janine di Giovanni, Leah McGrath Goodman, and Damien Sharkov. "How Does ISIS Fund Its Reign of Terror?" *Newsweek*. Newsweek, 6 Nov. 2014. Web. 17 June 2015.

13. Ibid.

14. Ashley Fantz and Stika Shubert. "From Scottish Teen to ISIS Bride and Recruiter: The Aqsa Mahmood Story." *CNN*. Cable News Network, 24 Feb. 2015. Web. 17 June 2015.

15. Janine di Giovanni, Leah McGrath Goodman, and Damien Sharkov. "How Does ISIS Fund Its Reign of Terror?" *Newsweek*. Newsweek, 6 Nov. 2014. Web. 17 June 2015.

CHAPTER 8. EVALUATING ISIS'S FUTURE

1. Jim Acosta and Jeremy Diamond. "Obama ISIS Fight Request Sent to Congress." *CNN*. Cable News Network, 12 Feb. 2015. Web. 17 June 2015.

2. Michael Flynn, James Livingston, and Michael Smith. "Retired Generals: Be Afraid of ISIS." *CNN*. Cable News Network, 11 May 2015. Web. 17 June 2015.

3. "ISIS Fast Facts." *CNN*. Cable News Network, 9 June 2015. Web. 17 June 2015.

4. Tim Marcin. "ISIS Air Strikes: US-Led Raids Kill 2,000 in Syria Since September, Report Finds." *International Business Times*. IBT Media, 23 Apr. 2015. Web. 17 June 2015.

5. Hunter Walker. "The US Military Is Investigating Possible Civilian Casualties from Anti-ISIS Airstrikes." *Business Insider*. Business Insider, 13 Feb. 2015. Web. 17 June 2015.

6. Pamela Engel. "ISIS Leader Baghdadi Is Reportedly 'Unable to Move' after a Spinal Injury." *Business Insider*. Business Insider, 27 Apr. 2015. Web. 17 June 2015.

7. Josh Levs, Ed Payne, and Michael Pearson. "A Timeline of the Charlie Hebdo Terror Attack." *CNN*. Cable News Network, 9 Jan. 2015. Web. 17 June 2015.

8. Jim Acosta and Jeremy Diamond. "Obama ISIS Fight Request Sent to Congress." *CNN*. Cable News Network, 12 Feb. 2015. Web. 17 June 2015.

9. Lori Hinnant and Paul Schemm. "War with ISIS: 'Go Have a Drink. Don't Pray. It's Not Islam. Don't Give Your Life up for Nothing,' Former Militant Advises Would-Be Jihadists." *Independent*. Independent, 3 Feb. 2015. Web. 17 June 2015.

10. Heather Saul. "ISIS Leader: Is Militant Group Replacing Its 'Injured' Chief Abu Bakr al-Baghdadi with a Former Physics Teacher?" *Independent*. Independent, 23 Apr. 2015. Web. 17 June 2015.

11. Mark Piggott. "ISIS: 'New Leader' Is Former Physics Teacher Abu Alaa Afri Replacing Paralysed al-Baghdadi." *International Business Times*. IBT Media, 23 Apr. 2015. Web. 17 June 2015.

INDEX

ABOUT THE
AUTHOR

Katie Marsico is the author of more than 200 reference books for children and young adults. Prior to becoming a writer, she worked as an editor in school and library publishing. Marsico lives with her husband and children and enjoys researching and writing about a wide range of topics.